CSS *ALABAMA*
VS
USS *KEARSARGE*
Cherbourg 1864

MARK LARDAS

First published in Great Britain in 2011 by Osprey Publishing,
Midland House, West Way, Botley, Oxford, OX2 0PH, UK
44-02 23rd Street, Suite 219, Long Island City, NY 11101, USA
E-mail: info@ospreypublishing.com

OSPREY PUBLISHING IS PART OF THE OSPREY GROUP

A CIP catalog record for this book is available from the British Library

Print ISBN: 978 1 84908 492 5
PDF ebook ISBN: 978 1 84908 493 2
ePub ebook ISBN: 978 1 84908 894 7

Battlescene, cover art, and quarterdeck views by Peter Dennis
Profile and armament artwork by Peter Bull Art Studio
Page layout by Ken Vail Graphic Design, Cambridge, UK
Index by Alison Worthington
Typeset in Adobe Garamond
Maps by bounford.com
Originated by PDQ Digital Media Solutions
Printed in China through Bookbuilders

11 12 13 14 15   10 9 8 7 6 5 4 3 2 1

Osprey Publishing is supporting the Woodland Trust, the UK's leading woodland
conservation charity, by funding the dedication of trees.

www.ospreypublishing.com

Author's note

The following abbreviations indicate the sources of the illustrations
used in this volume:

LOC – Library of Congress, Washington, DC
NHHC – United States Navy Heritage and History Command,
    Washington, DC
USN – United States Navy
AC – Author's Collection

Author's dedication and acknowledgment

This book is dedicated to Stephen Kinnaman, a fellow modeler
and maritime historian. Stephen helped me with research, and
allowed me to use him as a sounding board for maritime issues as
I wrote this book. The result is a book that is stronger than would
otherwise have been possible. Any errors that may still remain are
entirely my responsibility.

Artist's note

Readers may care to note that the original paintings from which
the colour plates in this book were prepared are available for private
sale. All reproduction copyright whatsoever is retained by the
Publishers. All enquiries should be addressed to:

Peter Dennis, "Fieldhead," The Park, Mansfield,
Nottinghamshire NG18 2AT, or email magie.h@ntlworld.com

The Publishers regret that they can enter into no correspondence
upon this matter.

Conversions

The following may be of use in converting between US customary
and metric units:

1 mile = 1.6km
1 nautical mile = 1.85km
1lb = 0.45kg
1yd = 0.9m
1ft = 0.3m
1in = 2.54cm/25.4mm
1 gallon (US) = 3.8 liters
1 ton (US) = 0.9 tonnes
1 cwt (US) = 45.4kg

CONTENTS

INTRODUCTION

There was a holiday mood in Cherbourg that Sunday – June 19, 1864. The morning weather was perfect. It was the type of fine day seen in northern France when spring was passing into summer.

Several hundred Parisians had taken advantage of a new weekend excursion train from Paris to Cherbourg to spend Saturday on Cherbourg's beaches. Most had chosen to stay an extra day, skipping the train's return on Sunday morning. Among them was Édouard Manet, the French artist, one of the pioneers of Impressionism. Several British and French yachts were also in Cherbourg that morning. These included *Deerhound*, a British steam yacht that had steamed into Cherbourg on the Saturday, to pick up the owner, John Lancaster, and his family, who were vacationing in France. Like the Parisian beachgoers, it delayed its departure to await the events of that Sunday morning.

There were two other visitors to Cherbourg that day – the focus of everyone's attention. In the harbor, raising steam, was CSS *Alabama*. The most celebrated (or as the Yankee press would assert, notorious) raider of the Confederate States of America, it had entered Cherbourg a week earlier, on June 11. Its captain, Raphael Semmes, intended to drydock the ship, which was showing wear from a 22-month cruise in which it had captured 65 Yankee merchant vessels, and sunk a Union warship – USS *Hatteras* – off Galveston Island. The ship badly needed an overhaul; its hull was leaking and foul, and its steam engine needed a rebuild.

Semmes's hopes were dashed by French officials. When the ship was built, European governments had winked at assisting the Confederacy. A year earlier, in June 1863 when the Army of Northern Virginia was invading Pennsylvania, Semmes might have secured permission for the lengthy refit in French facilities. But by June 1864 most European nations, even tacitly friendly France, felt that a Northern victory

Édouard Manet's famous painting of CSS *Alabama* sinking after the battle of Cherbourg. Manet witnessed the battle from Cherbourg. (AC)

was inevitable. Unwilling to alienate the eventual victor, French officials stalled granting *Alabama* permission to refit in Cherbourg.

Time was not Semmes's ally. The longer he stayed in Cherbourg the more likely it was that Union cruisers would reach the port and bottle *Alabama* up. This had happened to Semmes's last command, *Sumter*, which had found itself trapped in Gibraltar by two superior Northern warships while the raider awaited permission for repairs. Rather than endure blockade or return to sea in a leaky, slow craft, Semmes opted for a bolder course.

Outside Cherbourg was the second visitor – the United States Navy first-class steam sloop USS *Kearsarge*. Almost the same size as *Alabama*, *Kearsarge* had a crew that was slightly larger, and mounted seven guns to *Alabama*'s eight. It was commanded by John Winslow, an officer who had served under Semmes during the Mexican–American War, when Semmes was first lieutenant of the frigate *Raritan*, and Winslow was a division officer.

Kearsarge had been protecting Northern interests in European waters for longer than *Alabama* had been at sea. It was one of the two Union warships that had blockaded *Sumter*, and it had vainly sought *Alabama* off the Azores the previous year. For the past six months, *Kearsarge* had cruised the French coast, attempting to keep

three other Confederate raiders, CSS *Florida*, *Georgia*, and *Rappahannock*, locked up in port. These ships were located in both Brest and Cherbourg, and as *Kearsarge* was forced to operate out of Flushing, a Belgian port (as France and Britain refused to fuel it on a regular basis), this blockade had proved an exercise in frustration. *Florida* and *Georgia* had escaped, undetected, while *Rappahannock* remained in port only because of mechanical difficulties.

Kearsarge was in Flushing on June 12, when it received word of *Alabama*'s arrival at Cherbourg the previous day. Winslow immediately raised steam and set out for the French port, arriving off Cherbourg on June 14. He was expecting a long, boring wait outside the port, similar to his experiences with *Florida* and *Georgia*, but a surprise awaited him: Semmes wanted to fight. Via a circuitous diplomatic path Semmes sent word to Winslow to expect *Alabama* outside Cherbourg on the following day – or June 16 at the latest.

Both captains began preparations for combat. However, the challenge match – something from an earlier era of sea combat – did not come off that day or the next. Coaling *Alabama* took longer than expected, and this task was not completed until June 17. The following day, Saturday, June 18, was unsuitable for a sea fight. Swollen seas would have caused both ships to roll badly. But on June 19, the seas were calmer, and the weather perfect. At 10.30am, *Alabama* raised anchor and began steaming out of harbor.

Over the preceding days word of the impending clash had spread, luring yachtsmen and Manet to Cherbourg to watch, inducing the weekend bathers from Paris to remain. The impending battle was viewed by the neutral observers as a spectator sport, albeit more violent than most sporting events – a blood-sport version of a prizefight.

The French government contributed to that illusion. It had negotiated with both parties to ensure the battle would take place at least 6 miles from shore, well outside the 3-mile limit of territorial waters that was observed at that time. France did not want stray shells landing on French soil, and the big guns of both warships would exceed a 3-mile range. A French ironclad, the *Couronne*, was on hand to enforce neutrality, almost like a prizefight referee.

Many residents and visitors decided to watch the show from shore, atop the seaside cliffs where they could observe an action only 6 miles away. More ambitious observers chose a closer seat. Harbor pilot boats and local fishing boats took paying customers. These boats and private yachts at Cherbourg preceded and followed *Alabama* as it steamed out of port at 10.00am that morning for its rendezvous with *Kearsarge* and history.

The second of only three duels between Confederate raiders and the Union cruisers sent to hunt them, it was the most evenly balanced, and the only one fought within sight of an appreciative audience. The battle closed the age of the wooden warship. It would be the last major sea fight where two major nations fielded wooden ships as first-line warships.

CHRONOLOGY

1860
December 20 South Carolina becomes the first state to secede from the United States.

1861
February 4 North and South Carolina, Georgia, Florida, Alabama, Mississippi, Louisiana, and Texas hold a constitutional convention in Montgomery, Alabama.

April 12 Fort Sumter fired upon by Confederate forces.

April 19 President Lincoln declares a blockade of Southern ports from South Carolina to Texas.

May 8 Confederate Secretary of the Navy Stephen R. Mallory orders James B. Bulloch to England to obtain warships for the Confederate Navy.

September 11 USS *Kearsarge* launched at the Portsmouth Navy Yard, New Hampshire.

October 10 USS *Wachusett* launched at the Boston Navy Yard, Massachusetts.

1862
March 23 *Oreto* sails from Liverpool, England, for Nassau, Bahamas. Upon arrival, it is commissioned as CSS *Florida*.

August 24 CSS *Alabama* is armed and commissioned at sea off Terceira, Azores.

September 4 CSS *Florida* runs the blockade, arriving at Mobile, Alabama.

The ironclad CSS *Stonewall* was the Confederacy's greatest naval threat to the United States Navy, but United States diplomacy prevented its transfer to the Confederacy until it was too late for it to affect the course of the naval war. (LOC)

The *Alabama–Kearsarge* duel off Cherbourg, with *Kearsarge*'s aft pivot firing on *Alabama* during the battle. According to accounts from those aboard *Alabama* this gun did more damage than any other gun aboard *Kearsarge*. (LOC)

1863

January 11   USS *Hatteras* sunk by CSS *Alabama* in a battle off Galveston, Texas.

January 16   CSS *Florida*, outfitted in Mobile, Alabama, returns to sea, starting its first cruise.

September 17   CSS *Florida* arrives in Brest, France, after a 216-day cruise.

1864

February 10   CSS *Florida* sails from Brest, starting its second cruise.

June 19   CSS *Alabama* and USS *Kearsarge* battle off Cherbourg, France. After a 90-minute battle, *Alabama* is sunk.

October 7   CSS *Florida* captured by USS *Wachusett* while in a neutral port.

October 19   CSS *Shenandoah* commissioned off the Madeira Islands.

November 28   CSS *Florida* sunk in "accidental" collision in Chesapeake Bay.

1865

November 6   CSS *Shenandoah* arrives at Liverpool, England, and lowers Confederate flag for the last time. *Shenandoah* is later turned over to United States officials.

1894

February 2   USS *Kearsarge* wrecked on Roncador Reef off Central America.

1984

October 30   CSS *Alabama*'s wreck is discovered on the ocean bottom off Cherbourg.

DESIGN AND DEVELOPMENT

To a modern observer with a casual knowledge of ships, the oceangoing warships of the American Civil War appear little different from their counterparts of the War of 1812. At the end of the Civil War most seagoing warships were wooden-hulled, three-masted ships. The ironclad warships that began asserting dominance during the Civil War were still primarily coastal vessels. A few experimental seagoing ironclads had appeared, such as the British *Warrior* and French *La Gloire*, forerunners of the ships soon to dominate the oceans.

However, the sailing frigates of the War of 1812 had more in common with the warships of the 17th-century English Civil War than with the first-line warships of the American Civil War fought just 50 years later. By the 1860s, three revolutionary technologies had transformed naval architecture: steam power, iron construction, and percussion fuses. These technologies, not yet fully matured, had already profoundly altered warship design. Similarities with the previous generation of ships were superficial. The Confederate and Union cruisers that fought duels during the Civil War fought under steam power using large, shell-firing guns. Although they were planked with wood, iron reinforcement added strength, permitting longer, finer hulls.

Steam created the most visible change in ships since the War of 1812 – at least while the steam engines were running. The fuels used to fire the boilers of a steam engine created a distinctive column of smoke. The steam revolution started in the 1780s, with the first efforts to propel a ship using steam power, and the first successful steamboats appeared in the first decade of the 19th century. William Symington built *Charlotte Dundas* in Scotland in 1802, while in the United States Robert Fulton's *North River Steamboat* appeared in 1807. However neither of these was oceangoing:

USS *Constellation*, the last sailing warship built for the United States Navy, was already an anachronism when launched in 1856, but was typical of American warships in the first half of the 19th century. (USN)

Charlotte Dundas was a canal boat, while Fulton's boat was intended for the Hudson River.

Maritime steam grew quickly though. Fulton designed a steam warship, *Demelogos*, during the War of 1812, and in 1819 the Atlantic was crossed under steam power for the first time by the paddle steamer *Savannah*. Regular steam services across the Atlantic began in 1838, with *Great Western*, and by the Civil War steam was regularly used to ship high-value or time-sensitive goods across the ocean.

Naval use of steam initially followed at a slower pace. Steam freed warships from the wind, but the first generations of steamships used paddle-wheel propulsion. The large and fragile paddle boxes were vulnerable targets. Navies initially used steamships as auxiliaries – as tugs, for example – but paddle-steam warships began appearing in the 1830s. The real breakthrough came with the introduction of the screw propeller, which also appeared in the 1830s. Located below the waterline, propellers offered smaller targets, and, better still, they were more efficient than paddle-wheels. By the 1840s the screw steamship had become the standard warship.

Steam technology still had one major drawback in the 1860s: fuel consumption was too high. Thus, steamships, even warships, retained their sails for cruising. Although the sails were furled and the topmasts struck when a ship went into action, wind still offered free propulsion. But the steam engines and bunker space for fuel consumed much of the space that had previously been used for guns and stores.

Artillery advances mitigated the loss of gun-deck area. A revolution in naval gunnery had begun in the 1780s with the introduction of the carronade – a short-barreled cannon that threw a much larger ball than other guns of comparable barrel weight. The carronade was built to tighter tolerances than conventional artillery, and had innovations that reduced barrel weight and improved performance. It led to a reevaluation of artillery. By the first decade of the 19th century the naval gun was beginning to be transformed.

Large shell-firing guns – like this 9in Dahlgren being exercised during the Civil War – profoundly affected warship design. (USN)

One major change involved the caliber of shot. At the end of the 18th century, the heaviest cannonball in general use weighed around 32lb – a weight that could be comfortably handled by a single man on a rolling deck. Before carronades, only the largest warships were capable of mounting cannon firing 32lb shot, and these 32-pounders could be placed only on their lower gun decks. Lighter guns, firing lighter shot, were placed on the higher decks and in smaller warships. But all but the very smallest warships could carry the 32-pounder carronade and they were light enough to be placed on the forecastles and poops of large warships.

Artillery manufacturers realized that the principles used in the carronade could be used elsewhere. Shortening the barrel reduced the weight. The shorter-barreled gun lacked the muzzle energy of the long gun, but had at least as much hitting power as long cannon of the same barrel weight with a smaller bore. A medium-length 32-pounder was as effective as a long 24-pounder, while a short 32-pounder could outperform the long 12-pounder with a similar barrel weight. Carrying one size of ball simplified logistics, and by the 1820s many navies were refitting their ships to carry one caliber of gun, generally firing 32lb shot. Additionally, gunners were experimenting with using heavier shot, from 68lb all the way up to 150lb. Although it brought difficulties in handling the heavier shot, the increase in kinetic energy it offered gave larger guns an advantage over lighter ones.

Two other trends began emerging after the end of the War of 1812 – explosive shell and rifled cannon. Shells – hollow cannonballs filled with an explosive charge – had existed virtually as long as artillery, but their naval use was limited by fuse technology. Prior to 1800 shells had used timed fuses, generally involving a combustible wick. These proved impractical for sea service, except in very limited cases, such as mortars used only when anchored. In the early 19th century, mercury fulminate allowed emergence of the percussion fuse. This ignited on impact, triggering the explosive in the shell.

By the 1830s most navies had begun using shells. In the battle of Campeche, fought between the navies of the Republic of Texas and Mexico in 1843, both sides used explosive shells. The still-primitive fuses were so unreliable that the battle – fought at long range – ended indecisively. Ten years later, in 1853, explosive shells came of age, when a Russian fleet blew its Turkish opponents to splinters at Sinop using shellfire. Over the next decade, this trend accelerated, with all navies, including the United States Navy, developing guns designed to fire shells.

The greater size of shot and explosive power of shells increased the destructiveness of a single hit. In turn, that increased the importance of firing accuracy. In the 18th century warships depended upon high volumes of shot, fired at extremely short range (generally 50 yards or less) to batter opponents into submission. By the War of 1812, forward-thinking captains were training their crews to actually aim the guns at the enemy, rather than simply blazing away in the enemy's general direction, hoping some shots would hit.

Throughout the next part of the 19th century, leading up to the Civil War, navies worked on improving accuracy. While sights, gunnery tables and practice contributed significantly to increasing the percentage of hits landed, the use of smoothbore cannon limited the level of accuracy possible. Rifling the barrel – adding grooves that caused the projectile to spin – improved the accuracy of shot fired. But muzzle-loading rifled cannon took much longer to load than smoothbores. Breech-loading cannon had appeared in the 1850s, but at the start of the Civil War getting a good seal at the breech with the large-caliber guns preferred for their destructive ability was still extremely difficult.

Thus, by the start of the Civil War, most naval guns were smoothbore and muzzle-loading. Ships might have a few rifled guns for long-distance fire, but these were generally also muzzle-loaders.

Naval transition to steam was measured. The first generation of United States Navy steamships used paddle-wheels. Shown here is USS *Mississippi* during the Mexican–American War. (AC)

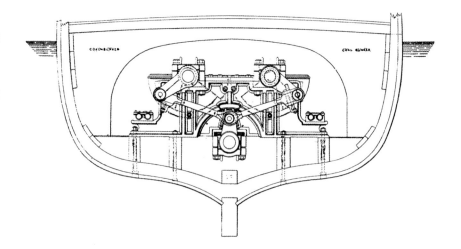

The revolution in ship structure began shortly before the War of 1812. While the least visible of the changes, it was the most important because it allowed the construction of larger hulls. Large-caliber shell-firing guns and steam propulsion required hulls of greater volume, both to contain the steam plant and fuel bunkers and to provide the buoyancy to support the greater weight of the artillery.

In the 1760s, a 100-gun ship-of-the-line – the largest warship built – displaced around 2,200 tons. The 74-gun ship-of-the-line, the standard ship used in line of battle, was between 160ft and 170ft long, 45ft to 50ft in beam and displaced between 1,600 and 1,650 tons. A frigate – the standard cruising warship – was 120ft to 130ft long and displaced between 600 and 700 tons.

By contrast, the last sailing warships built for the United States Navy were much larger. USS *Ohio*, the last 74-gun ship-of the-line built during the sailing era, was 197ft long and displaced 2,754 tons. The last sailing frigate, USS *Congress*, was 179ft long, 46½ft wide and displaced 1,867 tons – larger than the previous century's ship-of-the-line. Steam warships were bigger still. The Merrimack-class steam frigates were over 250ft long and displaced over 4,600 tons. All had wooden hulls, but none could have been built using 18th-century shipbuilding techniques. Two technical innovations permitted this increase – diagonal bracing and iron framing.

Prior to the 19th century, ships had been built with transverse frames connected to a longitudinal keel. This limited ships to a maximum length of about 180ft; any longer and the ship would work itself apart. The Constitution class of frigates, started in 1794, exceeded that limit when their designer, Joshua Humphries, added diagonal riders to the hull. Robert Seppings, Surveyor of the Royal Navy, independently developed a system of diagonal bracing adopted by the Royal Navy in 1811. Diagonal riders created a box-truss arrangement that increased the rigidity of the hull. It also reduced the 'working' of the hull – twisting during rough seas. Working weakened the timbers and allowed water to leak into the hull. Diagonal bracing was used in most large ships built after 1812 and retrofitted into ships built before then.

Concurrently with the introduction of diagonal bracing came the use of iron for ship structure. This was initially motivated by timber shortages, especially structural timber used in framing a ship. The most critical shortage was that of compass timber – curved pieces of wood used for the knees that connected beams to the frames. It took over a century to grow a tree large enough to produce these knees, and each tree had to be grown in an open field to allow its branches to spread.

Iron knees began to replace wooden knees in the first decade of the 1800s, and the use of iron quickly spread to other structural elements such as brackets, riders, and stanchions. Eventually, especially in Europe, where timber shortages were more severe, iron began replacing wood in the framing. The result was composite ships, which had an iron framework that was sheathed in wood. Even in the United States, with still-abundant supplies of timber, iron was used for knees, brackets and riders. The wooden warships of the Civil War were framed or reinforced with iron. By the 1840s iron-hulled ships had begun to appear, in both Europe and the United States. These trends would culminate in 1859 with the appearance of HMS *Warrior*, an iron-hulled, screw-propelled steamship with a battery of large shell-firing guns.

In the 1850s and 1860s wood still held some advantages over iron as a hull material. The iron then used was brittle, and would often shatter when struck by solid shot that would just punch a small hole through wood. Another issue was marine fouling. Wooden ships could sheath the underwater hull with copper, discouraging growth of marine life on the underwater hull. Iron ships could not do this without creating galvanic corrosion issues, as no adequate anti-fouling coatings existed in 1860.

While the cold waters of the North Atlantic minimized marine growth, taking an iron-hulled ship into warm tropical waters quickly gave a ship's bottom an ecology that would delight a marine biologist. Warm tropical waters also accelerated salt-water corrosion. New types of iron and steel developed after the Civil War alleviated brittleness and corrosion issues, but mid-19th-century navies had good reasons to prefer wooden walls.

USS *Lancaster*, one of the Hartford-class sloops, represented the current state of warship design in the decade prior to the Civil War. It still relied on its broadside rather than a pair of large pivots. (AC)

Designed by George Steers and built for speed, USS *Niagara* was as large as a World War I light cruiser. Useless for blockade duty due to its deep draft, it hunted Confederate raiders overseas. It is shown here at Antwerp, in 1864. (AC)

These revolutions in propulsion, armament, and ship structure had not been resolved by the time of the Civil War. As a result the naval war was fought with a bewildering assortment of ships, representing the lessons of the past 30 years. Both the Union and Confederate navies would employ virtually every type of ship developed since 1800 – from sailing frigates to armored ironclads. Some ships used sail, others paddle-wheels and others screw propellers. Some were wood or composite, while others were iron-hulled. But by 1860 an optimum ship type had developed for cruising warships used by both the Union and the Confederacy.

The best cruisers were screw steamers displacing 1,000 to 1,500 tons, between 180ft and 220ft long, with a beam between 30ft and 35ft. Because the ships were intended to spend long periods at sea, away from dockyards, the ideal cruiser had a wood-planked hull over iron or wood-and-iron framing. The hull contained enough volume to hold the machinery and crew quarters, with sufficient extra room for the stores needed to keep the ship at sea for several months, ammunition to fight several major battles, and enough coal to run the steam plant for three to four days at full power.

The steam plant, located amidships, consisted of direct-acting, low-pressure engines that had two or three cylinders generating between 500 and 700hp. At full steam the engines could drive the ship at speeds between 8 and 11 knots. The ship was also outfitted with a barque rig – a square-rigged fore and mainmast with fore-and-aft sails on the mizzenmast.

With the right wind, it could sail almost as fast under sail as with its engines alone. Using sail and steam combined, it could add another 20 to 25 percent to the top speed attainable under steam alone. At cruising speeds, under steam alone, a careful captain had coal enough for two to three weeks at sea; with judicious use of sail, a captain could remain at sea up to two months before running out of coal.

Cruisers generally had fewer than a dozen guns – six to eight was the norm. The most efficient arrangement placed two large guns amidships – one forward of the steam plant, and one behind it – and four to six smaller guns elsewhere on the gun deck. The two large guns were generally the largest guns that could be comfortably mounted on the cruiser, and were in centerline mounts, where they could be pivoted to either side of the ship. The smaller guns were often placed in broadside mountings. Often one light gun was mounted on the forecastle and one at the stern, on pivot mountings, as chase guns.

Exceptions to this general pattern occurred, caused by operational exigencies or simple happenstance. Within this framework, the Union and Confederacy came up with different solutions.

THE UNION CRUISER

For the United States Navy its war against Confederate raiders was a come-as-you-are affair. Despite the rapid expansion of the Union Navy during the American Civil War the Union Navy built no warships specifically intended to hunt Confederate commerce raiders. Only prewar designs and wartime conversions were available. Some were better suited to this purpose than others.

The most important classes of purpose-built warships available to the Union Navy were the steam frigates authorized in 1854 (the Merrimack class and USS *Niagara*), the Hartford-class screw sloops authorized in 1857, and the screw sloops authorized in 1859 (USS *Pawnee* and three different variants of the Mohican class). All were screw steamers, using propellers for propulsion, and intended to fight under steam power. Although the oldest group, the Merrimack-class frigates, were officially viewed as auxiliary steamers (implying that the steam engines were a back-up to sails), even these were measured by their performance under steam rather than as sailers.

All were designed to carry large-caliber shell-firing guns. While the earliest classes were designed to carry broadsides – ten to 20 guns on a side – their guns were much larger than those intended for the final generations of sailing frigates and sloops.

USS *Kearsarge* reflected final American thinking on wooden cruisers. It had a powerful steam plant, could cruise under sail, and carried two of the Navy's largest guns in pivot mounts. (LOC)

The frigates were built to mount a mixed battery of 9in Dahlgren smoothbores and 8in shell-firing guns on the upper deck. The Hartford-class sloops were built to carry 9in Dahlgrens and the 1859 sloops were built specifically to carry two 11in Dahlgrens. By the Civil War, these batteries were augmented with larger guns. *Niagara* was refitted with 12 11in Dahlgrens, while several of the Hartfords replaced guns with 11in Dahlgrens or 100-pounder rifles.

They were all conventionally constructed, from oak, with transverse framing, similar to ships of an earlier generation, like USS *Constitution*. Iron riders and wooden trusses installed diagonally added strength to the hull, allowing much larger ships than had been possible in 1800. *Niagara*, the largest, was 344ft long and displaced as much as a World War I light cruiser. Even the smallest – the 1859 sloops – were nearly 200ft long.

These ships were built for speed. The earliest – the 1854 frigates – were expected to steam at 9 knots using just their steam engines. When they failed to achieve those speeds they were viewed as semi-failures. The subsequent Hartfords were smaller, displacing two-thirds the volume of the frigates and with two-thirds the horsepower. The 1859 sloops were smaller still, but had engines that were as powerful as those of the Hartford class. While the five 1857 sloops averaged 9 knots under steam alone, the newer sloops, authorized in 1859, passed 11 knots on trials. Several almost reached 12 knots. Only *Niagara*, with engines twice the size of the other 1854 frigates, could keep up with the Mohican-class sloops.

The United States Navy also had screw steamers USS *Princeton* and *San Jacinto*, and paddle steamers USS *Mississippi*, *Allegany*, *Powatan*, *Saranac*, and *Susquehanna* that could be used as cruising warships. All had been built in the 1840s. Although elderly, they were still useful warships.

Finally, some purchased merchant vessels were turned into warships capable of hunting commerce raiders. The best example was USS *Vanderbilt*, a large paddle-wheel steamer built for Cornelius Vanderbilt as an Atlantic liner prior to the Civil War. Donated to the United States Navy after the war started, this iron-hulled ship carried a battery similar to those of the Hartford-class sloops of war.

Several of the available warships had liabilities limiting their usefulness as commerce raider-hunting cruisers. The surviving Merrimack-class frigates were too slow. Additionally they, like the 1840s ships (except *San Jacinto*) and the Hartford-class sloops, were fuel hogs. At full power the frigates burned between 2,600lb and 3,400lb of coal each hour. The Hartford-class sloops burned over a ton of coal per hour. When operating off the North American coast, where coal was readily available, this did not pose a real drawback; however coal consumption did create issues on remote stations. Neutral nations were allowed to provide coal to an individual combatant warship only once a month. Even then, a neutral was supposed to sell only enough coal to allow that ship to reach a home port. But with Europe containing numerous different nations, a ship could rotate from port to port across borders. Although some nations – such as Belgium – were willing to sell coal more frequently and in greater quantities than was permissible under strict interpretations of neutrality, fuel efficiency was still a major consideration in posting a ship overseas. That worked against the steam frigates, the paddle-wheel steamers and, to a lesser extent, the large Hartford-class sloops.

Another consideration was the need for powerful warships in American waters. The large batteries of the steam frigates and large sloops were ideal for shore bombardment – especially when opposing a shore battery – but were overkill when dealing with a lone Confederate commerce raider. Commerce protection was a secondary concern of the United States Navy during the Civil War, which focused on retaking control of the portions of the United States in rebellion against the central government. The large warships were assigned to local duties, rather than commerce protection.

There were exceptions. USS *Lancaster*, a Hartford-class sloop, and *Saranac*, an 1840s-era paddle steamer, spent the Civil War on the Pacific coast. These ships were at that station when the war started, and remained there. While a long way from the theater of war, the ships were operated mostly out of American Pacific ports rather than neutral ports.

The ships most frequently assigned to hunt commerce raiders overseas were the 1859 sloops (economical ships with a heavy punch), the *San Jacinto* and the lone fast steam frigate, *Niagara*, augmented occasionally by ships temporarily assigned to hunt specific raiders. Additionally, in the Gulf of Mexico or off the Atlantic coast – especially near the Bahamas or Bermuda – a Confederate raider might encounter a Hartford-class warship. Nearer the coast, a Confederate raider might meet a ship of a blockading squadron. This might be a powerful ship: *Sumter* had to outrun *Brooklyn*, a Hartford-class sloop. Equally, it might be a converted merchant ship that was totally outclassed by a true warship: that was the fate of *Hatteras*.

Elsewhere a Confederate raider would be most likely to encounter one of the ten smaller sloops of war – the Mohican-class vessels or *Pawnee*. Well over a dozen contacts between Confederate raiders and Union cruisers would involve one of these Union sloops. Most ended indecisively, two in combat.

Another cruiser routinely used to hunt Confederate raiders, USS *Tuscarora* was instrumental in trapping CSS *Sumter* at Gibraltar. It is off Gibraltar in this photograph. [AC]

USS *KEARSARGE*

Length between perpendiculars: 201ft 4in
Length overall: 220ft
Extreme breadth: 33ft 10in
Depth of hold: 16ft
Draft: 14ft 3in
Displacement: 1,032 tons
Complement: 166 officers and men
Machinery: One two-cylinder horizontal back-acting engine
  – 54in diameter × 30in stroke cylinder generating 307hp
  (UK calculation) or 822 NHP (USN calculation)
Armament at battle: Two 11in 133-pounder Dahlgren
  smoothbores, one 4.2in 30-pounder Parrott rifle, four
  short (32cwt) 32-pounder smoothbore cannon.
  Total weight of broadside: 360lb
Launched: Portsmouth Navy Yard, Portsmouth,
  New Hampshire, September 11, 1861
Commissioned: Portsmouth Navy Yard, Portsmouth,
  New Hampshire, January 24, 1862
Disposal: Wrecked, Roncador Reef, February 2, 1894

USS *Kearsarge* was one of four war-construction Mohican-class sloops of war authorized in 1861 as a wartime emergency measure. *Kearsarge* spent most of the war hunting Confederate raiders in European waters, sailing for the Azores almost immediately after being commissioned, returning in late 1864. During that period it participated in hunts for *Alabama* and *Florida*, and blockaded several other Confederate raiders, including *Sumter*, *Georgia*, and *Rappahannock* in different European ports. Having defeated *Alabama*, *Kearsarge* became a prestige command in the United States Navy, spending its postwar career on overseas cruises showing the flag. It ran aground on Roncador Reef, 225 miles east of Nicaragua, in 1894. Despite efforts the ship could not be salvaged, and was stricken from the Navy List that year.

THE CONFEDERATE RAIDER

The Confederacy's first problem using commerce raiders was obtaining them. Both CSS *Sumter* and CSS *Nashville*, two civilian steamers converted into the Confederate Navy's first commerce raiders, demonstrated that not every steamship was suitable for commerce raiding. *Sumter* was designed to carry passengers and express freight between New Orleans and Havana – a four- to five-day trip at moderate speeds – while *Nashville* was a passenger liner, intended for quick passages from port to port, and a side-wheel steamship, with vulnerable paddle boxes. Although both ships, especially *Sumter*, completed successful cruises, their shortcomings limited their usefulness.

Their biggest shortcoming was range. *Sumter* could cruise the Caribbean, which had multiple islands where it could make frequent stops for fuel, and could cross the Atlantic Ocean without loitering. However it could not park on distant sea lanes, waiting for prey. Frequent coaling stops increased chances that it would be found in port by a Union cruiser.

Another weakness was a lack of self-sufficiency. Both *Sumter* and *Nashville* had been built in the expectation that they would receive regular maintenance in harbor following relatively brief periods at sea. A successful commerce raider had to operate independently over long periods. The relatively light scantlings with which they had been built were incapable of carrying heavy guns. *Nashville* mounted only two 12-pounder smoothbores – enough to scare a merchantman into surrender, but not to fight a warship. Yet both ships showed the potential commerce raiding offered – if conducted by suitable ships.

The Confederacy lacked adequate shipyards. The only place that ships suitable for commerce raiding could be found was Europe, especially Britain. In spring 1861,

Not all Confederate raiders successfully got to sea. CSS *Alexandra* was seized by the British government before it could sail. Obviously a warship (note the gun ports), it violated Britain's Foreign Enlistment Act, limiting naval exports. (NHHC)

CSS *Florida* was the first of two wooden cruisers built for the Confederacy by Laird's shipyard in Liverpool. Along with *Alabama* it proved an apogee of raider design. (AC)

the Confederacy sent James Bulloch to England, tasking him with obtaining commerce raiders – through purchase or construction.

Bulloch sought ships large enough to carry supplies for three to six months at sea, as well as enough coal to allow them to steam continuously for two to three weeks. They also had to carry a battery heavy enough to meet most potential naval opponents on relatively even terms. Finally, they had to be able to cruise for prolonged periods – a year or perhaps longer – without the attentions of a first-class dockyard. Required maintenance had to be within the capabilities of a small yard in a minor port. This meant that wooden-hulled ships were preferable to those built from iron.

Screw propulsion was also required. Paddle steamers could be swift and were highly maneuverable – by backing one wheel and driving the wheel on the opposite side a paddle steamer could turn virtually in place. Most blockade runners were paddle steamers for that reason. But blockade runners were built to run, not fight. The large paddle boxes were large and fragile targets. A propeller, located below the waterline, was harder to hit.

Some merchant ships were suitable for conversion to raiders. Ships built for the China trade – voyages to and from Britain and the Orient – operated under conditions similar to that of a raider. They had to sail from Britain to China or Japan and back again with minimal maintenance. While they would normally make coaling stops along the way, they needed to carry enough coal to steam for at least two weeks between stops. They also needed to be swift enough and large enough to carry sufficient cargo to make their run profitable. Merchant ships with those characteristics were surprisingly similar in speed and dimensions to the standard cruising warships of the period – between 180ft and 230ft long, with a displacement between 700 and 1,200 tons and a top speed under steam of around 8 knots. Add guns to such a ship and you have a cruiser.

The Confederacy successfully purchased and converted some China trade ships into raiders. The most noteworthy example – CSS *Shenandoah*, a raider that took 38 prizes – began life as *Sea King*, built to transport troops and commercial cargos to the Far East.

CSS *Shenandoah* was the Confederacy's last cruiser. It was purchased, rather than built as a cruiser, but shared many characteristics with ships like *Alabama* and *Florida*. (AC)

These ships had an important limitation: their scantlings were typically lighter than those of a warship's. Shipbuilders constructed ships as economically as possible. Storm seas in winter North Atlantic waters or the Roaring Forties put significant strain on a hull. Since a China trade ship had to pass both the North Atlantic (including during the winter) and through the Roaring Forties, these ships had scantlings sturdy enough to weather these hazards. But even these hulls were not typically built to withstand the greater strain that the recoil of a firing gun created. By the 1850s, merchant vessels – even Indiamen – were not typically armed. A ship designed as a warship, built with heavier scantlings, made a better commerce raider than one designed as a merchant ship – even a vessel built for the China trade.

Used warships available for purchase in Britain were scarce – especially those capable of being used as raiders. If the Royal Navy disposed of a warship, or refused delivery of a ship newly constructed for its use, that usually indicated that the ship had problems. The Confederate Navy successfully purchased one used warship during the Civil War – HMS *Victor*, built in 1857 and sold in 1863; it was renamed CSS *Rappahannock*. The ship seemed perfect as a raider – it was wooden-hulled, the right size (857 tons, and 200ft long), and could carry a respectable battery. The reason the Royal Navy had disposed of it became obvious once it was at sea, when engine failures repeatedly forced the ship back to port.

The best raiders would be ships designed and built as warships. However, Britain's 1819 Foreign Enlistment Act forbade the sale of warships to belligerent powers; and although Britain refused to grant diplomatic recognition to the Confederacy, it did recognize it as a belligerent. To commission the construction of a ship capable of being a warship, the Confederacy had to order it for ostensibly commercial purposes. Once at sea, it could be outfitted with artillery, and converted to a warship. Bulloch successfully negotiated contracts for several warships under this pretext. Two – the ships that became *Florida* and *Alabama* – were successfully built and sent to sea. A third – intended as *Alexandra* – was seized during construction.

23

CSS *ALABAMA*

Length between perpendiculars: 213ft 8in
Length overall: 220ft
Extreme breadth: 31ft 8in
Depth of hold: 18ft
Draft: 17ft 8in
Displacement: 1,050 tons
Complement: 145 officers and men
Machinery: One two-cylinder direct-acting steam engine –
   56in diameter × 27in stroke cylinders producing 300hp
   (UK calculation) or 860 NHP (USN calculation)
Armament at battle: One 7in 100-pounder Blakely rifle,
   one 8in 68-pounder Blakely smoothbore, six long
   (55cwt) 32-pounder smoothbore cannon. Total weight
   of broadside: 396lb
Launched: Birkenhead Iron Works, Liverpool, England,
   May 14, 1862
Commissioned: Off Terceira Island, the Azores,
   August 24, 1862
Disposal: Sunk in combat, off Cherbourg, France,
   June 19, 1864

CSS *Alabama* was the most successful Confederate raider of the American Civil War and perhaps the finest example of a long-range cruising warship of that period. Built by the Birkenhead Iron Works under contract to the Confederate Navy, *Alabama* was designed for one function – to serve as a commerce raider capable of operating independently in an environment where it would receive little or no logistical support. It filled that role superbly.

Under the command of Raphael Semmes – who had proved himself a daring and skilled raider while captain of CSS *Sumter* – *Alabama* stalked United States-flagged merchant ships for 22 months. It captured 65 merchant vessels, burning 52, ransoming ten, and converting one into another raider, renaming it *Tuscaloosa*. One other ship captured in neutral waters was released, and one sold. It also sank USS *Hatteras*, the only Union warship lost to a Confederate warship in open waters.

THE STRATEGIC SITUATION

When the Southern states formed the Confederate States of America, they lacked a navy. The expected fight to secure independence was initially viewed as purely a land-based struggle. Navies were expensive, money was tight, and the Confederacy needed an army to repel Northern aggression. Naval forces might be useful for coastal defense, including keeping Southern ports open, but, at least at first, little thought was given to oceangoing warships.

The challenges faced by the United States Navy were at least as great as those faced by the Confederacy. In March 1861 the United States Navy had only 50 serviceable warships. Nearly half were on foreign stations, 40 percent lacked steam propulsion, and one-quarter of the steamers used paddle-wheel propulsion. Its resources were inadequate for the task of blockading the Atlantic and Gulf coasts from Virginia to

Alabama burning a prize. Early in its career, the fires from burning prizes attracted other victims, who would sail to assist a distressed ship. (AC)

Commander Newland Maffitt took command of *Florida* in Nassau, and successfully ran the Union blockade of Mobile, Alabama to outfit the cruiser in that port. (AC)

the Mexican border. Additionally the United States Navy still had responsibility for protecting the oceangoing American merchant fleet.

The Confederate government knew that warships could not be built in large enough numbers to seriously challenge the United States Navy on blue waters. The Confederacy lacked shipyards that could build enough seagoing ships to match even the prewar Union Navy, despite its capture of the Norfolk Navy Yard in 1861. Foreign purchases of warships would be difficult, even after European powers recognized the Confederacy as a belligerent power. British law forbade the sale of warships to belligerent nations, as well as the enlisting of crews for foreign warships in British ports. Although other European nations lacked those restrictions, the Confederacy could still not afford to purchase many warships. What resources the Confederacy initially expended on its Navy went towards ships intended to operate on coastal waters and rivers.

Despite an initial lack of warships, the South possessed several hundred trained naval officers. Deciding their loyalties lay with their state, 126 United States Navy officers holding commissioned rank had resigned their commissions and "gone South." Once a Confederate Navy was established, these men formed the core of its officer corps. Most were given assignments building shore batteries, or commanding coastal vessels.

Raphael Semmes was dissatisfied with that role. Having convinced Stephen Mallory, the Confederate Secretary of the Navy, to permit him to convert a merchant ship into a commerce raider, Semmes converted *Habana*, a 500-ton steam packet that in peacetime had sailed between New Orleans and Havana, into a warship. Rechristened *Sumter*, the ship was armed with one 8in pivot gun and four 32-pounder smoothbores.

Sumter sailed from New Orleans on June 19, 1861, running the Union Navy's blockade, and barely avoiding capture. Once at sea, the ship cruised the Gulf of Mexico and Caribbean Sea for five months, capturing twelve merchant vessels. Union Navy ships were sent in pursuit, but Semmes evaded them. By November, the ship needed a refit. Unwilling to run the blockade in the worn-out ship, Semmes took *Sumter* across the Atlantic, capturing another six prizes. The ship reached Cadiz, Spain, in January 1862, but Semmes was unable to get permission for a refit. *Sumter* moved to Gibraltar, where it was blockaded by Union cruisers, and again was unable to get repairs. It was sold out of Confederate service in December 1862.

The next Confederate raider to take to the sea was *Nashville*. It was converted from a paddle-wheel passenger steamer, and proved less adequate than *Sumter*. Sailing on October 21, 1861, from Charleston, South Carolina, it captured only two prizes on a four-month cruise, and was then sold.

Mallory was already attempting to obtain ships designed and built as warships. He had sent a delegation to Europe, headed by James Bulloch, to secure ships and naval supplies for the Confederate Navy. The main roadblock to Confederate hopes was Britain's pesky Foreign Enlistment Act, but Bulloch found a loophole. The Act not only allowed the construction of merchant vessels for belligerent powers, it also permitted the sale of weapons, including naval artillery. Bulloch placed contracts for ships ostensibly to be used as unarmed vessels, but suitable for conversion to warships. The guns and ammunition were purchased separately, to be added to the ship after it had left British waters.

The concept skirted illegality, but worked well enough to get several ships constructed. The first two – which became the Confederate raiders *Florida* and *Alabama* – were successfully built and taken to sea in 1862, despite attempts to get the ships seized by the British government. *Florida* – then called *Oreto* – was briefly detained in the Bahamas. After its release, the unarmed ship received its guns, but lacked both the crew and carriages to mount them. As it now obviously violated the Foreign Enlistment Act, its captain, Newland Maffitt, left the Bahamas and ran into Mobile, Alabama. There, *Florida* installed its battery.

Alabama managed to escape British waters mere hours before a writ confining her to Liverpool reached the shipyard that built her. Bulloch was less fortunate with other cruisers that he had built. *Alexandra* was detained by British authorities, on suspicion of violating the Foreign Enlistment Act, until the war ended. Two rams, built by Laird's shipyard, obviously warships, suffered the same fate. They were ultimately purchased by the Royal Navy. Three other British-built steamers, intended for China trade, were successfully bought by the Confederacy in 1863 and 1864 – again ostensibly as merchant craft – and converted to warships, armed outside British waters. They became the cruisers *Georgia*, *Rappahannock*, and *Shenandoah*.

All Confederate raiders suffered from a major weakness, regardless of their quality as warships. They lacked access to repair and maintenance facilities. Brilliant diplomacy by the United States's ambassador to Britain, Charles Francis Adams, and constant pressure by the United States government kept neutral nations from permitting Confederate warships to refit in dockyards controlled by the European powers. Damage and normal wear that reduced the ships' effectiveness could not be made good. Even coal was difficult to obtain. Often, United States diplomats would purchase all of the coal available in ports visited by Confederate raiders, to deny raiders coal even within the limits permitted by international law. Diplomacy did more than naval power to mitigate Confederate sea power.

Meanwhile the Union Navy committed itself to rapid expansion of both the available hulls and personnel. It purchased every available civilian ship that was suitable for conversion. Generally that meant any ship with steam propulsion, capable of mounting guns. Many carried only two or three guns, enough armament to stop unarmed blockade runners, and sufficient to hold off a Confederate warship long enough for aid to come from a larger, purpose-built ship. It also conducted a massive construction program, building 36 seagoing wooden warships to aid the blockade, and 39 paddle steamers intended for use on rivers and coastal waters. By December 1861, the United States Navy had 264 vessels of all types, manned by 22,000 sailors. It would continue to grow throughout the war.

Despite this expansion, the United States Navy was hard pressed. It had to blockade nearly 2,700 miles of Confederate coast and maintain a presence on several thousand

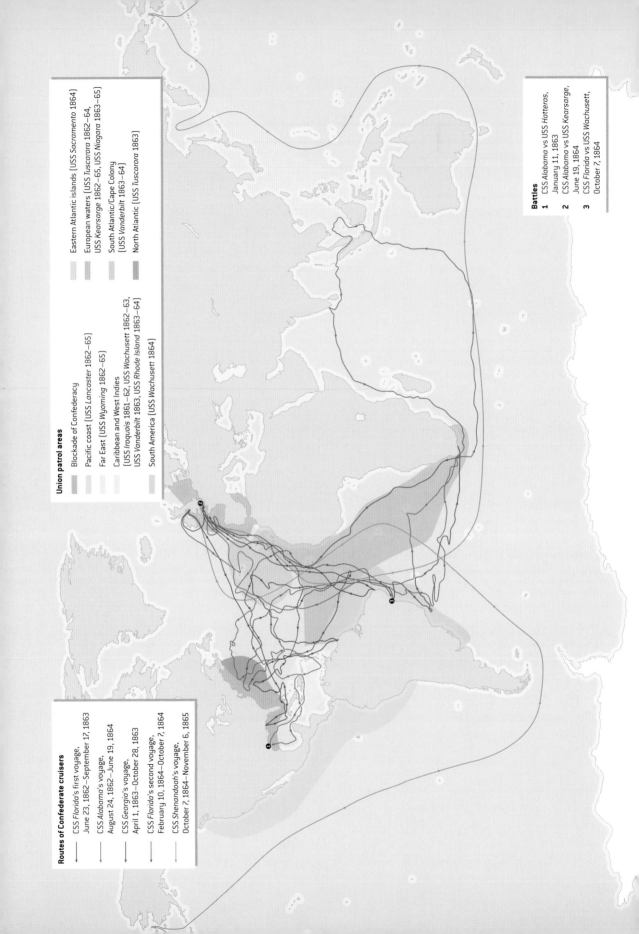

Routes of Confederate cruisers

→ CSS *Florida*'s first voyage,
June 23, 1862–September 17, 1863

→ CSS *Alabama*'s voyage,
August 24, 1862–June 19, 1864

→ CSS *Georgia*'s voyage,
April 1, 1863–October 28, 1863

⋯ CSS *Florida*'s second voyage,
February 10, 1864–October 7, 1864

— CSS *Shenandoah*'s voyage,
October 7, 1864–November 6, 1865

Union patrol areas

Blockade of Confederacy

Pacific coast (USS *Lancaster* 1862–65)

Far East (USS *Wyoming* 1862–65)

Caribbean and West Indies
(USS *Iroquois* 1861–62, USS *Wachusett* 1862–63,
USS *Vanderbilt* 1863, USS *Rhode Island* 1863–64)

South America (USS *Wachusett* 1864)

Eastern Atlantic islands (USS *Sacramento* 1864)

European waters (USS *Tuscarora* 1862–64,
USS *Kearsarge* 1862–65, USS *Niagara* 1863–65)

South Atlantic/Cape Colony
(USS *Vanderbilt* 1863–64)

North Atlantic (USS *Tuscarora* 1863)

Battles

1 CSS *Alabama* vs USS *Hatteras*,
January 11, 1863

2 CSS *Alabama* vs USS *Kearsarge*,
June 19, 1864

3 CSS *Florida* vs USS *Wachusett*,
October 7, 1864

In 1863 the Navy Department sent USS *Vanderbilt* in search of *Alabama*. Large and heavily armed, it would have been more than a match for the raider, despite its side-wheel propulsion. *Vanderbilt* never found *Alabama*, despite sailing to South Africa to seek it. (USN)

miles of inland rivers. Even after abandoning antislavery patrols off Africa, it was unable to maintain prewar strength on foreign stations. Including pure sailing warships, rarely were more than a dozen major warships overseas at any point in the war.

Generally these were parceled out in small numbers. Two ships covered the American Pacific Coast, one or two were in the Orient, a couple looked after the South Atlantic off Brazil, and one to three were assigned to European waters, including the Azores, Canaries, and Cape Verde Islands. The Caribbean was covered (when necessary) by the Gulf Squadron, focused on the Southern Blockade. Bermuda and the Bahamas were patrolled by the Atlantic Squadron, with an eye towards catching blockade runners more than raiders.

If a Confederate cruiser got to sea, the Navy Department might dispatch a ship or two extra to hunt it down. Three ships were sent after *Sumter* when that ship was in the Caribbean; the paddle-wheel cruiser *Vanderbilt* was sent to pursue *Alabama* in 1863; and *Wachusett* and *Kearsarge* were dispatched after *Florida* in 1864. The responsibility for catching raiders was usually given to the ship or ships on the foreign station where the raiders were thought to be. In early 1864 *Kearsarge* was given the single-handed task of keeping three Confederate raiders in widely separated French ports from sailing.

Navy Department policy assigned low priority to hunting raiders. The American merchant fleet was not critical to victory; maintaining the blockade and starving out the Confederacy was. Every ship sent hunting raiders was one less available for the blockade.

Meanwhile the Confederate raiders, sticking to their mission of destroying American commerce, avoided these Union cruisers. It was easy to do – the ocean was big and the raiders kept on the move. Even when caught in port, they would wait until favorable conditions allowed them to escape undetected. It is not remarkable that there were just three battles between Confederate raiders and Union cruisers; rather, it is surprising that there were so many.

TECHNICAL SPECIFICATIONS

Five ships were involved in the three single-ship duels during the Civil War: Confederate cruisers *Alabama* and *Florida*, and Union warships *Hatteras*, *Kearsarge*, and *Wachusett*. Four – *Alabama*, *Florida*, *Kearsarge*, and *Wachusett* – had been built as warships and were similar in construction and intended use. The fifth, *Hatteras*, was a coastal steamer, built to carry freight and passengers. It was one of many ships purchased by the Navy in 1861 and converted to a warship.

ARMAMENT

Alabama and *Florida* used similar patterns in the layout of their guns: the two largest guns were mounted on centerline pivots where they could be brought to bear on either broadside. *Alabama*'s pivots were a 7in Blakely rifle and an 8in smoothbore, while *Florida*'s were two 7in Blakely rifles. The rest of the Confederate batteries were broadside mounts, in trucked carriages – 32-pounder smoothbores for *Alabama* and 6in Blakely rifles for *Florida*. One or two of these were arranged so that the guns could be shifted from one side of the ship to the other. *Alabama* could shift two of its six 32-pounders to its engaged side for a broadside of four 32-pounder guns.

The Union ships were more variously arranged. *Kearsarge* had its two large guns on centerline pivot mounts amidships. It also mounted a light Parrott rifle on a pivot mount on the forecastle, and two trucked 32-pounder smoothbores on each broadside. *Wachusett* had three large guns, and six light guns. Two of the large guns,

100-pounder Parrott rifles, were in broadside mounts, while one was on a centerline pivot. It also mounted light Parrott pivots at the bow and stern, and four 32-pounder smoothbores on trucked broadside mounts. *Hatteras* had a similar arrangement with pivots at the bow and stern and four 32-pounder smoothbores in broadside carriages. *Hatteras* carried only light guns. It had a 30-pounder Parrott rifle and a 20-pounder Parrott rifle as pivots, a legacy of its civilian origins. *Hatteras* could not mount the heavy smashers that purpose-built warships could carry.

All of the guns carried in these battles were muzzle-loading, roughly evenly split between smoothbore and rifled barrels. Breech-loading cannon had appeared by 1860, but none were used by either the Confederate or the Union navies. Bulloch had attempted to purchase a 110-pounder rifled breechloader manufactured by Armstrong, but none were available because the Royal Navy had first call. The United States Navy focused on muzzle-loading guns because contemporary breechloaders had other drawbacks besides unavailability. Reliable means of sealing the breech on large guns had not yet been perfected. Breechloaders also used smaller charges for fear of breech failure.

The 7in Blakely rifles carried by *Alabama* and *Florida* fired cylindrical 100lb solid steel bolts or an 85lb shell up to 4 nautical miles. This was the extreme range of these guns, and hitting a target at that range would require more luck than skill. The barrels were 120in long, and weighed 7,800lb. For rifling they had nine square grooves with a right-hand twist. The six 6in Blakely rifles aboard *Florida* were the only 6in Blakely rifles built for naval service. They fired solid bolts that weighed 70lb or a shell that weighed 52lb.

Alabama running down a large, side-wheel merchant ship. *Alabama* was swift enough to catch even fast steamers. (AC)

WEAPONS OF *ALABAMA* AND *KEARSARGE*

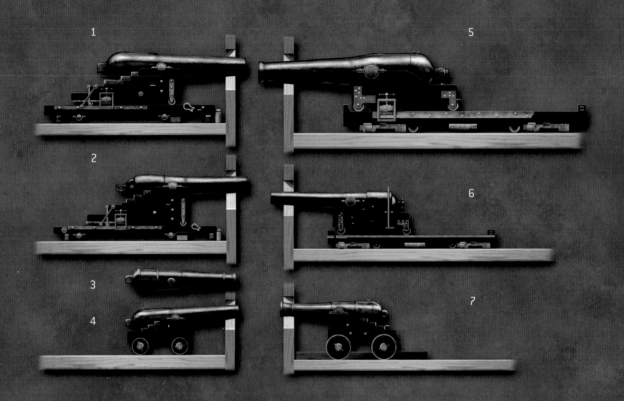

CSS *Alabama* carried eight guns and USS *Kearsarge* seven at the battle of Cherbourg. *Alabama*'s most reliable heavy weapon was its 8in Blakely smoothbore cannon (**1**). It fired a 68lb shot or a 42lb shell. *Alabama* also mounted a 7in Blakely rifled muzzle-loader (**2**). While this had a smaller bore, it carried a longer, larger round than the 8in smoothbore. Its shot weighed 100lb and a shell around 85lb. This gun had the longest range of any gun used during the battle, but took longer to load and tended to overheat under sustained periods of fire. Both guns were on pivot mounts, the 7in forward and the 8in aft of the engine room.

Opposing these two guns were *Kearsarge*'s two 11in Dahlgrens (**5**). These were smoothbore muzzle-loading cannon designed to fire shells. This type of gun normally fired a 133lb shell but was capable of firing a 166lb solid shot. Both were mounted on centerline pivots.

In addition to these large guns, *Kearsarge* mounted a 30-pounder Parrott rifle on its forecastle (**6**). This gun had a bore of 4.2in, and weighed 3,550lb. It was used as a chase gun, due to the long range of rifled cannon. This gun was operated by *Kearsarge*'s Marine contingent.

Both ships carried 32-pounder smoothbore cannon, on trucked carriages. *Alabama* had six long 32-pounders, with barrels that weighed 57cwt (6,400lb). Four (**4**) were new, manufactured by Fawcett-Preston. Two others (**3**) had been cast earlier (probably in the 1840s), but were available. *Kearsarge* had four 32-pounders (**7**), short 32cwt guns (approximately 3,600lb).

MOVING A PIVOT GUN

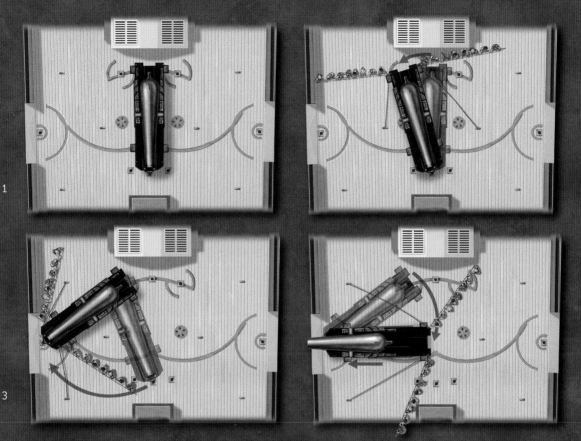

This illustration depicts the operation of one of *Alabama*'s pivot guns, but the principle was much the same on other ships. While the pivot mount allowed a gun to be stored on the centerline of a ship (improving cruising stability) and could be used off either broadside (halving the guns required) getting a large pivot into position was an involved job.

Each pivot mount had pivot pins at the front and back of the carriage. When stowed amidships, both pins were set, holding the gun in position (**1**). The first step in moving the gun to its firing position was to remove the pin at the rear pivot point. That allowed the gun to pivot about the front pivot pin. The gun crew would then pull the rear of the carriage, swinging it so that the rear of the carriage was over a new pivot point, closer to the ship's side (**2**).

The rear pin would be dropped, fixing the rear of the carriage at the new pivot point, and the front pivot pin removed. This allowed the carriage to rotate about the rear pivot point. The gun crew would pull on lines at the front of the carriage, moving the front of the carriage to the firing position (**3**).

The front pin would be dropped into the firing position pivot, and the rear pin removed. This allowed the gun crew to pull tackles at the back of the carriage and rotate the gun into its firing position (**4**).

Alabama's 8in Blakely was a smoothbore. It fired spherical shot that weighed 68lb or shells that weighed 42lb loaded. All Blakely guns were constructed with a cast-iron barrel to which wrought-iron or steel bands were added to reinforce the breech. This allowed greater breech pressure than would have been possible otherwise.

Kearsarge carried two 11in Dahlgren smoothbores. These were massive guns. Designed by John Dahlgren, the Dahlgren gun had a milk-bottle shape with a fat breech and a tapered muzzle. Its one-piece cast iron barrel was 160in long, and weighed 15,700lb. It fired a 166lb solid shot or a 133lb shell; with a 10lb charge, and elevated 8 degrees, it could fire a shell 2,300 yards. A shell was capable of penetrating 4½in of iron armor backed with 20in of oak.

Wachusett used 100-pounder Parrott rifles for its main battery. Parrott rifles used a slender cast-iron barrel with a wrought-iron band shrunk around the breech. The result was a strong gun that could be produced quickly and relatively inexpensively. The naval 100-pounder Parrott had a 6.4in bore, with a barrel that was 130in long and weighed 9,700lb. It was rifled with five grooves. With a 10lb charge, elevated 8 degrees, it could send a 100lb shot or shell 2,800 yards.

Kearsarge, *Wachusett*, and *Hatteras* also carried smaller 20-pounder and 30-pounder Parrott rifles. The 20-pounder Parrott had a 3.67in bore, with a barrel that was 79in long, weighed 1,750lb, and had five rifling grooves. The 30-pounder Parrott had a 4.2in bore, seven rifling grooves and a 96in-long barrel that weighed 3,550lb. It used a 3½lb gunpowder charge, and at 10 degrees it had a range of 3,640 yards. The grooves of all Parrott rifles were ⅒in deep.

The final gun carried by both sides was the 32-pounder smoothbore. These guns had a 6.4in bore, and fired a solid shot that weighed 32lb or a 21lb shell. Built from essentially

the same design that had been in use for nearly a century, by the middle of the 19th century these guns had less windage (the difference between the gun's bore and the diameter of the ball) than earlier versions. Additionally, the barrels were being cast in different lengths with different weights that ranged from 32cwt to 61cwt. The Union ships in these battles carried light 32-pounders, while *Alabama* mounted 57cwt 32-pounders.

One of the two older 32-pounders carried on *Alabama*. This gun was recovered from the sea bottom off Cherbourg in 2009. (USN)

STRUCTURE

Four of the five ships involved in single-ship duels were designed as warships. *Florida* was based upon a design for a British dispatch vessel, *Alabama* a gunboat. The two Union sloops of war, *Kearsarge* and *Wachusett*, were two members of a class of ten screw-steam sloops of war designed by the United States Navy in the late 1850s. Intended as multi-function warships, these ships were capable of supporting operations in coastal waters, but also able to operate independently, protecting American interests at remote stations. One function for which they were designed was hunting commerce raiders. All but one of these ten ships saw extended service on remote stations during the Civil War.

All four ships had a high length-to-breadth ratio. *Alabama* was 210ft long and had a maximum beam of 32ft for a length-to-breadth ratio of 6.7:1. *Florida* was 191ft long with a 27ft beam, and a length-to-breadth ratio of 7:1. The two Union sloops were a tad portlier with a length-to-breadth ratio of 6:1. (By contrast *Constitution* has a length-to-breadth ratio of 3.9:1.) These longer, slenderer hulls were made possible

Alabama's main punch lay in its two large pivots. Raphael Semmes can be seen leaning on Alabama's 8in Blakely. Behind him is John McIntosh Kell, Alabama's first lieutenant. (NHHC)

by advances in ship construction between 1800 and 1860, but it was necessary to build hulls of those proportions in order to accommodate a steam engine, allow space for deck space for guns and still produce a ship capable of moving swiftly.

The Mohican class represented a ship designed around its intended main battery – its two 11in Dahlgrens. The guns required an 18ft carriage, and an 11in Dahlgren on its carriage weighed 20,000lb. Each gun required a deck footprint between 20ft and 24ft in length. The ship's machinery required 50ft of length. Placing guns as heavy as the 11in Dahlgren close to the bow or stern promoted hogging – a condition caused when excessive weight and insufficient buoyancy at the ends of the ship pull the bow and stern of a ship down, while water pushes the middle up.

Hogging caused a ship's keel to curve down like a banana, stressing the upper decks, and weakening the ship's hull. Adding a long bow and stern to the midsection carrying the main battery and engines eliminated hogging; additionally a long, thin hull produced less water resistance than a shorter hull of the same displacement. The resulting hull form could carry heavy guns yet move quickly. While the Confederate cruisers did not carry a battery as heavy as that intended for *Kearsarge* or *Wachusett*, these principles led to a similar hull shape. Speed was useful for the Union ships – it was a necessity for *Alabama* and *Florida*.

All four warships were constructed in a remarkably similar manner. All were wooden hulled ships, reinforced with iron riders and knees. The Confederate ships were built from elm, oak, fir, and teak; their keel and strakes were elm, their scantlings oak, and their deck beams were Danzig fir. The Union warships were constructed from white oak, live oak, and pine. All were copper bottomed, with a layer of copper plates protecting the wooden hull from the teredo worms. The seemingly anachronistic wooden hull was appropriate for both navies. The United States had no shortage of wood, and wooden hulls were more easily maintained than iron ones. The Confederacy expected limited access to shipyard facilities, so the extra expense of building wooden ships in Britain was offset by the ease of maintenance.

The odd ship in this group was *Hatteras*. Iron hulled, it was originally built as a merchant steamer. It was 210ft long with a beam of 34ft and drew 18ft fully loaded. Incapable of carrying heavy guns, *Hatteras* was an adequate warship for its intended purpose of enforcing the blockade; it was not intended to battle regular warships. Even its iron-hulled construction worked against it. *Hatteras*'s structural iron was typical of its day – strong but brittle. Struck by solid shot, *Hatteras*'s hull plates were likely to fail catastrophically, shattering rather than yielding a shot-sized hole.

PROPULSION

All combatants of the battles in this book used steam propulsion during combat, although all were equipped with sails. Sails were viewed as auxiliary propulsion, to be used to augment steam power when wind could be used advantageously. The Confederate raiders, lacking reliable coal supply, tended to use sails more frequently than their Union counterparts.

Alabama and *Florida* were both equipped with direct-acting horizontal steam engines built by Fawcett and Preston of Liverpool, England. A direct-action engine drove the propeller (or paddle-wheel) shaft directly from the cylinder piston rods. Horizontal engines had the pistons set horizontally, keeping more of the piston below

HORSEPOWER

Those familiar with sources listing technical details of the Confederate raiders may notice that *Alabama* and *Florida* are assigned horsepower values different than given in other works. The reason lies in different means of calculating Nominal Horse Power (NHP – a means of calculating the relative power of different steam plants) in the United States and Britain. The formula for NHP per cylinder is:

$$NHP = (\text{cylinder pressure (psi)} \times \text{piston area (in}^2) \times \text{piston speed (ft/min)})/33,000$$

The piston speed is the length of the stroke (in feet) multiplied by engine RPM.

In Britain, NHP was calculated at constant cylinder pressure – 7psi. The United States Navy used the working pressure of the cylinder – 12 to 20psi during the Civil War era. To keep everything constant, I have used United States Navy (USN) practice in all NHP calculations. The working pressure of *Alabama* was 20psi. By USN standards, *Alabama* had an NHP of 860hp rather than 300hp given in sources like Bowcock.

While essential, the steam engines of the Civil War era were complicated and frequently balky. This drawing shows the engine crew freeing a sticky connecting link. [AC]

the waterline. These engines turned the shaft at the same rate as the engine's stroke per minute – there was no gearing to allow the shaft to move faster or more slowly than the engine.

Both ships were equipped with two-cylinder engines, although *Florida's* engine was two-thirds the power of *Alabama's*. Each of *Florida's* cylinders produced 100hp as measured by Admiralty calculations, while *Alabama* had cylinders that produced 150hp. According to Admiralty rules the two engines of the ships had effective indicated horsepower of 667hp and 1,000hp respectively. By United States Navy measurement (USN), *Florida's* engine produced 571hp and *Alabama's* 857hp.

To allow better performance under sail, both ships were equipped with two-bladed propellers that could be disconnected when the engine was not in use, and hoisted out of the water into a well ahead of the rudder.

Kearsarge and *Wachusett* were equipped with two-cylinder back-acting steam engines. Back-acting engines also had horizontal cylinders, but the cylinder's piston rod was attached to a crankshaft with a return connecting rod driving the propeller shaft. They, too, were direct-drive engines turning the shaft at the same speed as the engine. *Kearsarge* had cylinders with a diameter of 54in; *Wachusett*'s cylinders were 50in. Both had a 30in stroke. *Kearsarge*'s plant yielded 822hp (USN), while *Wachusett*'s smaller engine produced 717hp (USN). Both had a maximum speed of 11.2 knots under steam power alone during sea trials.

The United States Navy outfitted both sloops with four-bladed propellers. More efficient than two-bladed screws, they could not be lifted out of the water. Instead these ships were equipped with clutches that allowed the propellers to be disconnected from the shaft and freewheel when the ship was under sail alone.

All four ships were equipped with barque rigs – the main and foremast were square rigged, while the mizzenmast had only fore-and-aft sails. In addition, the forward masts had booms and gaffs for fore-and-aft trysails. *Alabama* had a sail area of 14,661ft^2, while *Kearsarge* carried less than 9,700ft^2 during the Civil War.

Hatteras was a side-wheel paddle steamer, rather than a screw-propelled ship. It had a walking-beam steam engine that generated 500hp (USN). The pistons drove an overhead beam that had a second rod connected to a crankshaft that drove the paddle-wheel. Although a popular engine in the United States for paddle steamships, the engine was a vertical design that had numerous exposed parts, including the steam cylinder and the beam.

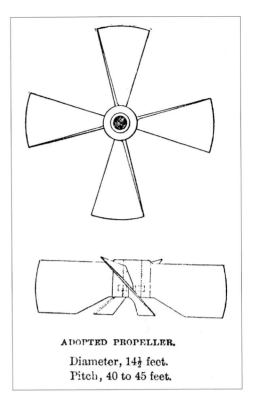

ADOPTED PROPELLER.
Diameter, 14½ feet.
Pitch, 40 to 45 feet.

A maritime screw propeller used by the 1860s United States Navy. A four-bladed propeller was more efficient than a two-bladed screw, but could not be hoisted out of the water. (AC)

THE COMBATANTS

Since the American Civil War was a civil war – a war fought between political factions or regions of the same country – it might be expected that the combatants had similar, if not identical backgrounds. This was certainly true of the officer corps of both sides, many of whom had served together on the same ships. The seamen who manned the ships of each side came from different nations; yet even here there were more similarities than differences.

THE OFFICERS

In 1860 the United States Navy had 1,563 officers. Of these 551 held commissions (captain, commander, or lieutenant), 53 were Marine officers, and the rest held staff or warrant ranks. Of this number, 321 "went South" – resigned from the US Navy and joined the armed forces of the Confederacy – 126 commissioned officers, 14 Marine officers, and 181 staff or warrant officers. Both navies drew their officers from that common pool. The five captains who commanded the warships that fought the three single-ship cruiser duels during the American Civil War had been shaped by similar experiences in prewar careers, and so had many of their subordinate officers.

From its inception in 1798 until the start of the Civil War, the United States Navy was a small and highly professional service. Between the end of the War of 1812 and the start of the Civil War it never exceeded a total manpower of 10,000 and never boasted more than 1,000 "line" officers, a category that included midshipmen, masters, and those holding commissions.

A line officer entered the prewar Navy as a midshipman, an officer in training. Prior to 1845, midshipmen served their apprenticeship aboard ships. There they learned basic seamanship, navigation, and the principles of commanding men. They berthed in the wardroom or cockpit, located in the middle of the ship – hence their name. By the 1820s a school had been established at Norfolk to provide education in the more academic aspects of being an officer, mathematics and navigation. This supplemented, but did not replace sea duty.

In 1845, Congress established the United States Naval Academy at Annapolis, Maryland, and much of the training of midshipmen was transferred there. Interestingly, however, none of the captains involved in the cruiser duels attended Annapolis.

After six years as a midshipman, the officer could stand for an examination that would qualify him to serve as a lieutenant. Passing did not immediately gain promotion to lieutenant; instead the officer became a "passed midshipman." A passed midshipman filled a role similar to an ensign in today's US Navy, serving many of the functions of a lieutenant without the commission.

The next step on the ladder of command was to serve as a master. Masters, originally responsible for the navigation and safety of the ship, had evolved into a form of non-commissioned lieutenant in the mid-19th-century United States Navy. They ranked below the commissioned ranks but above the other warrant officers, including midshipmen.

The next move was attaining commissioned rank – so called because commissioned officers held a commission issued by the United States Congress. The lowest commissioned rank was lieutenant. From there the progression was that of lieutenant commander, commander, and captain. At the start of the Civil War, there was no rank higher than captain, although a captain placed in charge of a squadron gained the courtesy title commodore. Both Union and Confederate navies established permanent flag ranks during the Civil War.

Originally the officers holding ranks of lieutenant commander, commander, and captain commanded ships of varying sizes. The only subordinate commissioned officers on ships were lieutenants. By the 1850s this had yielded to a new system where the executive officer on a ship – the role held by the first lieutenant during the War of 1812 – would be given to a commander on a ship that was a captain's command, or a lieutenant commander on a ship normally given to a commander. This offered more seagoing billets to men holding commander's commissions.

Service in the peacetime Navy was frequently interrupted by periods ashore as even with the small size of the officer corps there were more officers than active-duty stations, and fewer seagoing billets than active-duty assignments. Officers often spent years on leave or on shore assignments – recruiting, at a naval base, or as a lighthouse inspector – between periods of sea duty. A minimum of two years in any single grade was required before a man could be promoted to a higher

Charles M. Morris, *Florida*'s last captain, was typical of Confederate officers. Born in South Carolina, he served as an officer in the United States Navy for 24 years prior to resigning his commission in 1861 and joining the Confederate Navy. (NHHC)

rank, but in practice promotion was frequently much slower. Semmes spent 18 years as a lieutenant before becoming a commander, and John Winslow 16 years. Neither man, despite over 30 years of service, had reached captain by the start of the Civil War.

By the Civil War the Navy had a new type of commissioned officer – the staff officer. These men filled roles requiring specialized knowledge. They included surgeons, paymasters, chaplains, schoolmasters, and engineers. Originally these men held warrant ranks – outside the line of command, but ranking above the sailors and petty officers – but as the complexity of their tasks increased, so did their ranks. Eventually the men who practiced these specialist functions gained "assimilated" rank equivalent to a commissioned line officer, but outside the chain of command. Surgeons and paymasters were assimilated in the 1840s; in contrast, engineers – viewed as mere mechanics – were not assimilated until just before the Civil War. Each specialty followed a separate path for obtaining warrants, commissions, or promotions – thus the Navy's Bureau of Medicine and Surgery passed surgeons, while paymasters and engineers each had a department that conferred rank.

The newest category of officer was that of the engineers. These officers were responsible for the operation and maintenance of a ship's steam engines – one of the most important parts of the ship. However in these early days of steam technology, most engineers were self-taught, and more focused on the technical aspects of their jobs than on naval courtesies seen as important by line officers. Often they were tolerated rather than appreciated by the other officers. Despite this, by 1859 the United States Navy had established engineering ranks – chief engineers ranked as commanders, while third assistant engineers were the equivalent of midshipmen.

With secession, two navies were established. The United States Navy maintained its structure, adding volunteer ranks to support its massive expansion. The Confederate Navy mimicked the structure of its northern counterpart, transferring the rank structure and organization of the United States Navy. Enough line officers "went South" to provide the cadre for the Confederate raiders. Only 18 engineering officers transferred allegiance to the Confederacy, but since there were never more than four raiding cruisers in commission at one time, there were enough engineers to provide the officers to run their engines.

THE MEN

A naval sailor's life in the 1860s remained much the same as in the final wars of the Age of Sail. Many responsibilities remained unchanged. Sailors still handled the rigging, set the sails used for cruising, worked the guns, and steered the ship. Most of this work was still done as it had traditionally been done for centuries – with human muscle power. However, technological advances since the 1810s had added to the challenges of sailors' lives, and steam propulsion had created a new category of seaman – men who fed and ran the steam engines. This divided the crew into two categories – the deck sailors who filled the traditional role of sailors and the "black gang" who ran the engines.

The engineer, shown at his post in the engine room, was still a new breed of officer in the 1860s. By the Civil War deck officers had not yet decided what to make of engineers. (AC)

The deck force was divided into categories of landsmen, ordinary seamen, and seamen. Landsmen were those who knew little to nothing about ships; an ordinary seaman had mastered the fundamentals of seamanship, while a seaman was someone skilled in all of the traditional aspects of a sailor's trade. The engine-room counterparts to these ranks were coal-heaver, second-class fireman, and first-class fireman. Coal-heaver was the least skilled position, with responsibility for feeding the furnace with coal. The firemen had varying levels of responsibility for tending the boilers and watching the engines, under the supervision of the engineers – the officers responsible for the engines.

Above these seamen was a wide assortment of specialist ranks: painter, armorer, carpenter, and coxswain. There were also leading seamen called "captains" who had charge of different portions of the ship – captain of the hold, captain of the forecastle, captain of the afterguard. A ship also carried "boys" – youngsters in their teens who carried powder charges.

Pay reflected both skill and the difficulty of the job. The black gang – who worked under the most arduous conditions in the most technically challenging job on the ship – were the best-paid group. An unskilled coal-heaver received more pay than a seaman, while a second-class fireman was paid as much as a gunner's mate.

Life aboard ship had changed a little, but was essentially much like service 50 years earlier. Sailors still worked four-hour or two-hour watches. In the morning they washed the ship, scrubbing the decks and cleaning brightwork. Once a week the sailors added washing their clothing and hammocks to the morning routine. Afternoons were used for drill, (both gunnery and sail), equipment maintenance (overhauling rigging, checking over the guns, engine maintenance), and making and mending their clothing. Sundays were still a day of rest when possible.

RAPHAEL SEMMES

Raphael Semmes was born on September 27, 1809, on his parents' tobacco farm in Charles County, Maryland. His parents, Richard Thompson Semmes and Catherine Middleton Semmes, were fourth-generation Marylanders, drawn to the state because they were Roman Catholics. Although the family was prosperous, Raphael Semmes and his younger brother Samuel were orphaned at an early age.

The two boys were raised by his father's three brothers: Alexander, Benedict, and Raphael Semmes. Uncle Alexander was a shipowner and Uncle Raphael a merchant with interests in overseas trade. These two uncles fostered Raphael's interest in the sea, and in 1826 Uncle Benedict, a physician, secured a midshipman's warrant for his nephew Raphael.

Semmes spent much of the next six years at sea, in the midshipmen's mess aboard various naval warships, learning his trade. After acquiring the required six years of experience Semmes sat his examination, and passed it, becoming a passed midshipman.

Semmes spent much of the 1830s on half-pay. While awaiting assignment, he studied law and was admitted to the Maryland bar in 1834. Thereafter he intermittently practiced law. During one of those periods, he stayed in Cincinnati, Ohio, where he met Anne Elizabeth Spencer. They married in 1837, and would eventually have six children.

In 1836 Semmes commanded a small river steamboat during the Second Seminole War. The boat ran aground and was wrecked, but the incident did not mar his career, and in 1837 he was promoted to lieutenant.

The Mexican–American War saw Semmes commanding the brig *Somers*. In December 1846, he was on blockade duty off the Mexican coast when, as he chased a blockade runner, *Somers* was caught in a sudden squall and sank. Semmes was cleared of wrongdoing in the subsequent inquiry (*Somers* had a reputation as an unstable ship) and commended for his actions during the crisis. Afterwards, he was made first lieutenant of the sailing frigate *Raritan*, the squadron's flagship. Later, he participated in the invasion at Vera Cruz, commanding some of the guns sent ashore to provide support, and accompanied the army on its drive to Mexico City.

Following the war, Semmes wrote a book about his experiences: *Service Afloat and Ashore During the Mexican War*. The book, which appeared in 1851, became a bestseller, and made Semmes, briefly, a celebrity. By then Semmes had moved to the Alabama coast, eventually settling in Mobile.

His career developed less satisfactorily. Except for a brief period in 1848, when he commanded the storeship *Electra*, and in 1855 when he was given the mail steamer *Illinois*, he spent the period between the Mexican and Civil wars ashore, either unemployed or at shore postings. Most of his active service was on lighthouse boards, inspecting lighthouses on the American coast. He was promoted to commander in 1855, but often thought of abandoning the Navy.

There had been several positive changes in sailors' lives. Food was better: canned food and dried (desiccated) vegetables supplemented the salt food of an earlier age, and fresh food was available more often because ships made more frequent stops in port, in order to replace the coal that fed the steam plant. Fresh water was of better quality. It was now being stored in iron tanks rather than wooden barrels, reducing the growth of flora and fauna in the water. On steamships fresh water was more available; boilers required pure, salt-free water and steamers had water distillation plants aboard to produce this, with excess product available for crew consumption.

Captain Raphael Semmes shortly after the battle with *Kearsarge*. (AC)

a warship, renamed *Sumter*. He and his command proceeded to run the Union blockade, and began a six-month cruise in which *Sumter* captured 18 Yankee merchant ships.

By then *Sumter*'s steam engines required replacement. Unable to effect repairs, Semmes paid off the ship in Gibraltar. He was then given command of the newly completed *Alabama*, which he commanded on a cruise that lasted nearly two years. Before being defeated by *Kearsarge* off Cherbourg, Semmes and *Alabama* captured 64 Union merchant vessels and defeated USS *Hatteras*.

Semmes escaped capture after *Alabama* sank. While in Britain he wrote an account of *Alabama*'s cruise, before returning to the Confederacy via Cuba and Mexico. In late 1864 he was promoted to admiral, and given command of the James River Squadron, a small force of river craft guarding Richmond. When the capitol was abandoned, Semmes burned the boats and formed the squadron's personnel into a naval brigade attached to the Army of Northern Virginia.

After the war's end, he returned home to Mobile. Arrested by the United States government, he was charged with treason, piracy, and mistreating prisoners; however, the charges were dismissed before coming to trial. He briefly taught at Louisiana State University, and edited two newspapers, but lost all three positions. He then lectured and wrote *Service Afloat and Ashore During the War Between the States*, another bestselling book. He died in 1877, from food poisoning.

When the Deep South voted the articles of secession in 1861, Semmes decided his allegiance lay with Alabama rather than the United States or his birth state, Maryland. He was assigned to head the Confederate lighthouse board, but convinced the Confederate Secretary of the Navy to allow him to outfit a commerce raider instead. At New Orleans Semmes converted a Havana packet into

Another significant change was a reduction in the consumption of alcohol. Spirit rations were reduced from those of the earlier wars, and beer eliminated. Non-alcoholic beverages – tea, coffee, and cocoa – were substituted. Sailors were more sober than in previous generations, at least aboard ship. This was even truer after the United States eliminated the spirit ration in 1862. Confederate ships remained "wet" throughout the war.

Sailors still slept in hammocks, but these were roomier than they had been at the turn of the century. Navy hammocks were now 72in long and 30in wide. The extra space was possible because crew sizes were smaller. A 1,000-ton warship in 1814 had carried a crew of 300 men; by 1864 a crew of 160 was more typical for a ship of this

Despite changes – such as the addition of uniforms – sailors still lived in much the same way as they had 50 years earlier. The crew of a ship is shown relaxing during a "make and mend" afternoon. (Note the black sailors at right, repairing uniforms.) (AC)

displacement. In large part this was because of the trend towards small batteries of larger, deadlier guns; whereas a 1,000-ton frigate in 1814 had typically mounted 50 guns, the 1,000-ton Civil War sloops of war carried six to eight. The sloops were also significantly longer, creating more deck space for berthing, even after space for the engines and coal bunkers was subtracted.

Sailors faced additional hazards. Steam plants were dangerous places, even when everything worked properly. A slip could result in burns from contact with hot

By the start of the Civil War Marine contingents typically manned one of the ship's guns. Aboard *Kearsarge* – as shown here – the Marines manned the ship's forecastle 30-pounder Parrott rifle. (AC)

FOOD

The improvement in the quality of sailors' rations can be seen by comparing the Civil War ration with that of the War of 1812. A comparison of weight shows an apparent loss of quantity, but this is misleading. Desiccation, by removing water, significantly reduced the weights of vegetables, and canned meat lacked the bone and gristle found in salted meat of earlier eras.

Sailor's daily ration, United States Navy	
War of 1812	**Civil War (1861)**
Daily: • 1–1½lb salt beef with ½ pint rice or 1lb turnips, potatoes, or pudding, or • 1lb salt pork, ½ pint peas or beans, 4oz cheese or • 1lb salt fish, 2oz butter or 1 gill oil, and 1lb potatoes	Daily: • 1lb salt pork with ½ pint beans or peas, or • 1lb salt beef with ½lb flour, and 2lb dried apples or other dried fruit, or • ¾lb preserved meat, ½lb rice, 2oz butter, and 1oz desiccated vegetables, or • ¾lb preserved meat, 2oz butter, and 2oz desiccated potatoes
With: • 1lb bread, • ½ pint (8oz) distilled spirits or 1 quart beer	With: • 14oz biscuit (hard tack) • ¼oz tea or 1oz coffee or cocoa • 2oz sugar • 1 gill (4oz) of spirits
	Weekly: • ½lb pickles • ½ pint molasses • ½ pint vinegar

A note about the spirit ration: The Navy had not only cut the ration in half by 1861, but prohibited it to anyone under age 21. Underage sailors were paid the value of the spirit ration (5 cents – roughly one-eighth of a landsman's daily pay), as were those over 21 who chose to forego spirits. In 1862 Congress eliminated the spirit ration, replacing it with its equivalent value in pay.

machinery. Equipment failure – whether through wear, bad construction, or combat damage – could allow scalding steam to escape. The larger sizes of the cannon provided their own hazards: inattention could result in crushing injuries. Finally, explosive shells posed a danger both to the sailors handling them and to those at whom they were aimed.

Ships still carried Marine contingents (sea soldiers) although the boarding battles for which they were originally created had largely disappeared by the Civil War. Marines still served to maintain discipline aboard ship and to act as sentinels. They were still used for shore parties, but during seagoing actions they were generally assigned to work the guns, rather than as snipers. Sea battles were typically fought at

JOHN WINSLOW

John Ancrum Winslow, captain of *Kearsarge*, was born in Wilmington, North Carolina, on November 19, 1811. Nevertheless, he was a New England Yankee by upbringing and temperament. His father, also named John Winslow, was a member of a long-established Massachusetts family that traced its origins to the *Mayflower*. The senior Winslow moved to Wilmington for business reasons, but maintained strong connections with his native state.

When Winslow was in his early teens, his father sent the boy to Massachusetts for his education. There young John Winslow attended preparatory schools in Dorchester and Dedham. The youth developed a desire for a naval career, and in 1827, at age 16, he obtained an appointment to the United States Navy as a midshipman. His sponsor was Daniel Webster, a senator from Massachusetts.

Midshipman Winslow was assigned to the sailing sloop of war *Falmouth*, then newly launched. He spent six years aboard *Falmouth* learning his trade, remaining on Pacific cruises through most of this period, and became a passed midshipman in 1833; in this role, he went on to sail another two-year cruise in the South Atlantic.

Prior to departing for the South Atlantic, he became engaged to a cousin, Catherine Winslow, and they married on October 18, 1837, after his return. After spending the next two years on a shore duty, he was finally promoted to lieutenant in February 1839.

Captain John Winslow in his dress uniform. (AC)

Winslow's first decade as a lieutenant was typical of the careers of many United States Navy officers. A cruise aboard the schooner *Enterprise* on the Brazil station was followed by sick leave, more shore duty, and assignment

ranges greater than the effective range of rifles. Often, the Marines were assigned to one particular gun. On *Kearsarge*, the Marines manned the forecastle Parrott.

The major difference between the Confederate and Union navies was the source and make-up of their crews. Although sailors were an international breed, and the Union Navy had plenty of foreign sailors, most seamen aboard Union warships were residents of the United States – either citizens or immigrants. In contrast, aboard the Confederate cruisers most of the forecastle hands were foreigners.

This difference was largely due to recruiting. Ships had to be manned before they could be taken to sea, so both navies recruited from the places where they built or bought their ships as well as where they operated them. The Union purchased or built its ships along the northern Atlantic coast of the United States – Pennsylvania, New

to the steam frigate *Missouri*. He was aboard *Missouri* when it caught fire in Gibraltar, on August 26, 1843.

During the Mexican–American War, Winslow served aboard the sailing frigates *Cumberland* and *Raritan*. In October 1846 he commanded one of the flank landing parties during an assault on Tabasco, where his gallantry led to his being mentioned in dispatches by Commodore Matthew Perry. He also briefly commanded the dispatch boat *Morris*, but when *Morris* ran aground in a storm and was lost he was reassigned to the frigate *Raritan* as a division officer. Raphael Semmes was then the frigate's first lieutenant, having been placed there after losing his command.

Winslow served as first lieutenant of *Saratoga*, another sailing sloop of war, in 1848, then did a stint aboard *St Lawrence*, another sailing frigate, in its Pacific cruise from 1851 to 1855. After 1855 he was promoted to commander and served ashore for the next five years. At the outbreak of the Civil War he was inspector for the Second Lighthouse District, and was living in Boston, the district's headquarters.

An ardent abolitionist, Winslow applied for sea duty, and was sent to the Mississippi River Squadron, at Cairo, Illinois. He spent 18 months commanding river ironclads, but his service was undistinguished, interrupted by frequent illness, and dogged by misfortune. He was promoted to captain in July 1863, but remained on the rivers. Winslow asked for reassignment, but instead he was furloughed; finally, after sending another request for assignment, he was offered command of *Kearsarge*.

It was a curious assignment. Sloops like *Kearsarge* were normally given to commanders, not captains. The Navy Department may have made the offer to dispose of an undistinguished and troublesome officer. If Winslow refused he could expect no future offers. If he accepted, he would be occupying a remote post where he could do little damage.

Winslow accepted, joining *Kearsarge*, which was already on station in European waters, in April 1863. He spent the next year in a frustrating search for Confederate raiders, fruitlessly seeking *Alabama* off the Azores, and attempting single-handedly to blockade *Florida*, *Georgia*, and *Rappahannock* in French ports. His long wait ended in June 1864 when he fought and defeated *Alabama*. *Kearsarge* was relieved in the fall of 1864, and upon its return Winslow was a national hero. The Navy's previous misgivings about Winslow were forgotten, and he was promoted to commodore effective the date of the battle with *Alabama*, although Winslow was so high on the captains list that the advance was modest.

After the Civil War ended Winslow commanded the Gulf Squadron. He was promoted to admiral in 1870, and given command of the Pacific Squadron. However his always fragile health broke under this sea service. He was relieved for medical reasons, returned to Boston, and died there on September 29, 1873.

Jersey, New York, and the New England states. The Confederate raiders, however, were built or purchased in Britain.

The majority of the initial crews for Union cruisers came from coastline states. Most men who enlisted in the United States Navy at enlistment stations in inland states went to the rivers fleet. The United States Navy also allowed recruitment of black sailors, even prior to the Civil War. How many black sailors were aboard a ship often depended on where it served. *Kearsarge*, commissioned in New England in early 1862, spent most of the war in European waters and had only a few black sailors. Crews aboard cruisers on blockade duty in the South might be as much as 30 percent black.

In the United States Navy sailors enlisted for a fixed period of time. At the start of the war, the term of enlistment was three years, although by 1864 this had been

Men wanted
FOR
THE NAVY!

All able bodied men and boys

Will be enlisted into the NAVAL SERVICE

upon application at the Naval Rendezvous.

Come forward and serve your Country

WITHOUT CONSCRIPTION!

Roanoke Island, Dec. 8th, 1863.

ABOVE LEFT
One attraction of naval service was that it kept recruits out of conscripted service in the Army – a point emphasized in this recruiting poster. (NHHC)

ABOVE RIGHT
Ships carried a small percentage of teenaged youths on their rosters. Rated "boys," they were used to carry powder to the guns during action. (LOC)

shortened to one year. Thus there was a turnover of sailors, as enlistments expired. At the end of the Civil War, the United States Navy had 51,000 sailors, although as many as 132,000 different men may have served over that period.

The Confederate Navy filled its crews with sailors recruited in Europe, especially England. The Confederacy circumvented the Foreign Enlistment Act by enlisting sailors outside of British waters. *Alabama* was manned by sailors hired to take the ship to the Portuguese Azores, where it was commissioned as a warship. Similarly, *Georgia's* crew signed on off Brest, where that ship was armed. The Confederacy did not use black sailors in its Navy. The only black man aboard *Alabama* was a man from Delaware who was aboard a prize taken by the raider. Semmes seized the man as contraband property and he served as the officers' mess steward.

The result was that crews of Confederate ships contained a higher percentage of professional mariners than Union warships, which contained a large number of landsmen as a result of the massive expansion of the Union Navy. But Union crews proved no less professional or less courageous over the course of the war.

COMBAT

There were only three duels between Confederate raiders and Union cruisers during the Civil War. Admittedly, this was not for lack of effort on the part of Union captains. USS *Iroquois*, a near-sister to *Kearsarge* and *Wachusett*, found *Sumter* in Martinique. It waited outside the harbor for an opportunity to fight the raider, but *Sumter*, badly outclassed, slipped out, avoiding the Union warship. *Alabama*, similarly caught in Martinique by the screw frigate *San Jacinto*, contrived a similar escape. *Vanderbilt*, a side-wheel steamer donated to the Union Navy, and armed with two 100-pounder Parrott rifles and 12 9in Dahlgrens, was sent to hunt *Alabama* in January 1863. It searched in vain for nearly a year, almost catching the raider near the Cape of Good Hope, but failing when Semmes wisely took *Alabama* out of *Vanderbilt's* reach.

Blockading warships also had opportunities to catch several of the Confederate raiders as they slipped in and out of Southern ports. *Brooklyn*, one of the five 2,200-ton Hartford-class sloops of war, almost caught *Sumter* as it left New Orleans. A clean hull and a newly overhauled engine allowed the 500-ton *Sumter* – with a fraction of the 22-gun broadside of its larger foe – to escape capture. Similarly, *Florida* evaded Union blockaders to enter Mobile Bay in September 1862, exiting it in January 1863.

The problem faced by the Union captains was finding a Confederate raider captain willing to engage in a fight with them – or rather finding one willing to disregard his mission sufficiently to engage in a fight. Confederate captains wanted to fight warships in preference to simply capturing unarmed merchantmen. As much or as little as individual Confederate captains enjoyed destroying United States-flagged merchant ships (Semmes, for example, enjoyed this part of his job), naval glory was obtained by seeking out and destroying enemy warships. It was part of the tradition of the service in which they had spent their careers, and a tradition they wished to transplant to their new Navy.

In order to fight a Confederate raider you had to catch it. CSS *Sumter* is shown here evading USS *Brooklyn* off the Mississippi River's Outer Pass. (LOC)

But the Confederate captains were also aware that their ships were assets that were not easily replaced, that the commerce raiding which they were conducting was important to the Confederacy, and that the glory of defeating a Union cruiser had to be balanced against the risk to that mission. Thus, there were only three circumstances under which a commander of a Confederate raider would match arms with a Union cruiser: first, if the Confederate captain felt that he had a sufficient measure of superiority over his opponent to guarantee victory without serious risk to his own ship; secondly, if his ship – although in a place of safety – could not continue its mission without challenging an enemy warship; and finally, if combat were forced upon him. Each of the three single-ship duels that occurred illustrates one of these three circumstances.

OVERWHELMING SUPERIORITY: *ALABAMA* vs *HATTERAS*

January 11, 1863 found CSS *Alabama* off the Texas Gulf coast, 30 miles southeast of Galveston Island. In December, Raphael Semmes had learned that General Nathaniel Banks, commanding the Union Army in the Department of the Gulf, planned to send additional troops to Texas. The expedition was scheduled to arrive at Union-held Galveston on January 11.

The opportunity to destroy a convoy of transports filled with Yankees was too tempting to resist. Semmes calculated that with surprise he could sink a dozen – perhaps several dozen – transports before any escorting warships could interfere. The blow would strike directly at the Yankee military, rather than indirectly by attacking Northern shipping. The target was worth the risk of his ship in a way that even a victory over a Union warship was not.

Unknown to Semmes, a Confederate attack on Galveston on New Year's Day had recaptured the island. A combined force of troops and cotton-clad steamboats had captured all Union troops on Galveston, taken the warship USS *Harriet Lane* and destroyed another warship, USS *Westfield*. When the remnants of the Union squadron at Galveston reached New Orleans, Banks canceled his expedition. Admiral David Farragut, commanding United States Navy assets in the Gulf, dispatched his flag captain, Henry H. Bell, with *Brooklyn* and six gunboats, to Galveston to investigate. Instead of encountering a fleet of transports when Semmes approached Galveston on the afternoon of January 11, he found Bell's squadron of warships instead.

Semmes hauled up to assess the situation. The enemy squadron was hull down, but their masts clearly showed that they were warships. His lookouts counted five ships. While Semmes had come seeking a fight, he had no intention of battling five warships. Yet he was reluctant simply to leave. Then he saw an opportunity. His lookouts reported that one of the ships was leaving the squadron and sailing towards them.

Bell's lookouts had spotted *Alabama*'s masts just as *Alabama*'s had spotted those of the Union squadron. Bell detached one of his ships to investigate the strange sail. Preoccupied with Galveston and unaware that *Alabama* was in the Gulf of Mexico, Bell spent too little time considering the implications of that sail. He assumed that the ship was possibly a blockade runner that had heard about Galveston's new ownership, and never considered that it might be a Confederate warship. If he had, he would have gone himself, in the flagship *Brooklyn* – and possibly become the man that sank the *Alabama*.

Instead, he sent *Hatteras*, an iron-hulled side-wheel gunboat. Originally launched as the civilian steamer *St Mary*, it had been purchased into the US Navy during the 1861 expansion, and armed with six guns – a 20-pounder and 30-pounder Parrott rifle on pivot mounts and four 32-pounder smoothbores on broadside mounts. This was

Semmes planned his raid on Galveston when *Alabama* was spending Christmas at Arcas Keys. The crew is shown enjoying shore leave there on Christmas Day. (AC)

Alabama lured USS Hatteras away from a Union squadron, and then in a short, 13-minute battle off Galveston Island defeated the outclassed side-wheel warship. (NHHC)

adequate to overawe blockade runners, or fight cottonclad tugs armed with a 32-pounder or two – its usual foes – but not *Alabama*.

Semmes brought his boilers up to pressure, and engaged his engine, slowly sailing east, away from the squadron. He kept his speed low enough to allow his pursuer to draw near, but gradually increased the distance from the Union squadron. He did not recognize the oncoming ship, but realized that it was a purchased merchantman converted to a warship, rather than a purpose-built man-of-war – and that its broadside weight of metal was unlikely to exceed his own.

Hatteras's captain, Lieutenant Commander Homer C. Blake, was a regular officer whose United States Navy career had begun in 1840. As he drew nearer to the strange sail he recognized it was a steamer – and had the appearance of a warship. He also suspected that he was being lured away from *Hatteras*'s companions. *Hatteras* should have been slower than the strange ship it was overhauling, but it was not. Blake cleared *Hatteras* for action, and signaled his suspicions to *Brooklyn*. Either the signal was missed as dusk approached or it was ignored. *Hatteras* continued its chase alone.

By the time *Hatteras* came within hail of *Alabama*, it was dark and *Hatteras* was over 20 miles from the other Union warships. Blake hailed *Alabama* asking what ship it was; Semmes replied that it was an English warship. Semmes states that he claimed to be HMS *Petrel*; Blake reported that he was told the ship was HMS *Vixen*. In turn, Blake identified his ship, but Semmes failed to catch the name, only that it was a United States Navy warship.

Blake, unconvinced that the other ship was British, told Semmes that *Hatteras* was going to send a boat. Semmes waited until the boat was lowered, identified himself as the captain of CSS *Alabama* and opened fire. Almost instantly *Hatteras* returned fire. Between the two ships was *Hatteras*'s boat with six sailors and a master's mate aboard. They rowed out of the line of fire, remaining spectators through the rest of the fight.

The battle was fought at short range – 50 to 100 yards. *Hatteras* kept up a rapid rate of fire, hoping that gunfire would attract the attention of the nearby squadron. *Alabama* fired more deliberately, using its larger guns to deadly effect. Shells penetrated the hold, amidships in the wardroom and struck the engine, making it impossible to move *Hatteras* or run the fire pumps. After 12 minutes, *Hatteras* was sinking, *Alabama* was virtually undamaged. Recognizing that further resistance was futile, Blake flooded his magazine, fired a gun on the unengaged side, and hoisted a light on *Hatteras*, to indicate that he had struck.

Semmes steamed over to *Hatteras*, and asked if it had surrendered; Blake replied that it had. Semmes asked if assistance was needed, and, on being told that *Hatteras* was sinking, took the crew aboard *Alabama*. Soon after being evacuated, *Hatteras* settled to the shallow Gulf bottom.

The flashes of gunfire could be seen from Galveston roofs during the fight. While Bell's squadron heard gunfire, they were fogbound, unable to move until dawn. By the time they reached the site of the battle, *Alabama* had long since departed. The only things greeting them were *Hatteras*'s masts, sticking up from the water, and the boat lowered by *Hatteras*, with its seven-man crew.

FIGHTING TO CONTINUE THE MISSION: *ALABAMA* vs *KEARSARGE*

When CSS *Alabama* reached Cherbourg in June 1864, it was a significantly different ship than the one that had defeated *Hatteras*. *Alabama* in January 1863 was a ship at the peak of its career. It had been at sea for only four months – long enough to shake out any problems and train its crew to work as an effective team, but not long enough for fatigue to affect the ship's hull or engines.

The *Alabama* that entered Cherbourg had been cruising for 22 months without a break. The ship needed a dockyard refit – routinely done to most warships of that era every year to 18 months. Its hull was foul and leaked, its engines were worn, and its crew was weary after the long voyage. They wanted their pay and a stretch ashore. Even its officers were tired. Semmes originally planned to pay off his crew and put *Alabama* into drydock for refit for several months. Its hull would be cleaned and re-caulked, bad wood replaced, and its steam engines overhauled. A refit also offered a long run ashore for himself and his officers, and the chance for rest.

Semmes soon realized that this was impossible. The French had an endless list of reasons why his requests could not be satisfied. Cherbourg was a naval port – its dockyards were only for ships of the French Navy. Perhaps if *Alabama* had docked at Le Havre, a civilian port ... but neutrality laws prevented *Alabama* from reentering a

French port for another three months after departing Cherbourg. Semmes resented these new rules, which were a change from France's previous tacit support for the Confederacy.

The change recognized new realities. In 1862, when *Alabama* left Liverpool, the Confederacy had seemed on the verge of achieving independence. Emperor Napoleon III, France's ruler, had then withheld diplomatic recognition of the Confederacy only because he was unwilling to grant it unless Britain also did. By the spring of 1864, most European nations – even France – believed the Confederacy was losing. Aiding Semmes would anger the United States – which would be around long after the doomed Confederacy.

Semmes had three basic options – to keep *Alabama* in port to be blockaded, to return to sea with a slow, worn-out ship and a disaffected crew, or to challenge the first Union cruiser that reached Cherbourg. He opted for the last course.

Several goals fed into Semmes's decision. First, he believed the ship he would face would be *Kearsarge*. On paper the ships were evenly matched: they were the same size, and had almost the same number of guns and virtually the same broadside. *Kearsarge* was in better shape mechanically than *Alabama*, having just had its engines overhauled, but *Alabama*'s steam plant was up to the demand of a few hours of battle.

Secondly, if *Alabama* lost a single-ship duel, the overall situation for the Confederacy would not be significantly changed. It certainly would be no different than if *Alabama* lay idle in Cherbourg for the rest of the war – the most likely situation if Semmes waited and additional Union cruisers joined the blockade. On the other hand, if *Alabama* sank or took *Kearsarge*, especially if the action took place before the eyes of French and British witnesses, Semmes felt this might swing favor back to the Confederacy.

Semmes intended more than simply beating *Kearsarge*, however. He planned to board *Kearsarge*, overwhelm its crew – which would not expect a boarding action – and take the ship, virtually undamaged. Semmes would then transfer his crew to the new prize, and begin another raiding voyage on a fresh ship – refitted by the Yankees, no less. A gamble, yes – but Semmes had been gambling and winning from the day he took *Sumter* out of New Orleans.

Semmes sounded his executive officer, John McIntosh Kell, about fighting *Kearsarge*. Semmes had orders from the Confederate Navy Department to avoid combat with Union cruisers, but Kell, too, was eager to fight, and agreed that current conditions merited ignoring those orders. Semmes's final concern was whether the crew, who had grown restive during the trip to France, would be as willing to fight as he and *Alabama*'s officers were – but when he spoke to them, Semmes found they were as eager as he was for a final, decisive battle.

Kearsarge arrived at Cherbourg on June 14, steaming through the harbor to view its opponent, and then posting itself outside the harbor. Its crew was eager for a chance at the legendary Confederate "pirate." By then, Semmes had resolved to fight. He passed word of his intention to the Confederate envoy to France, who passed it to the French government. Eventually, Semmes's challenge reached John Winslow, commanding *Kearsarge*.

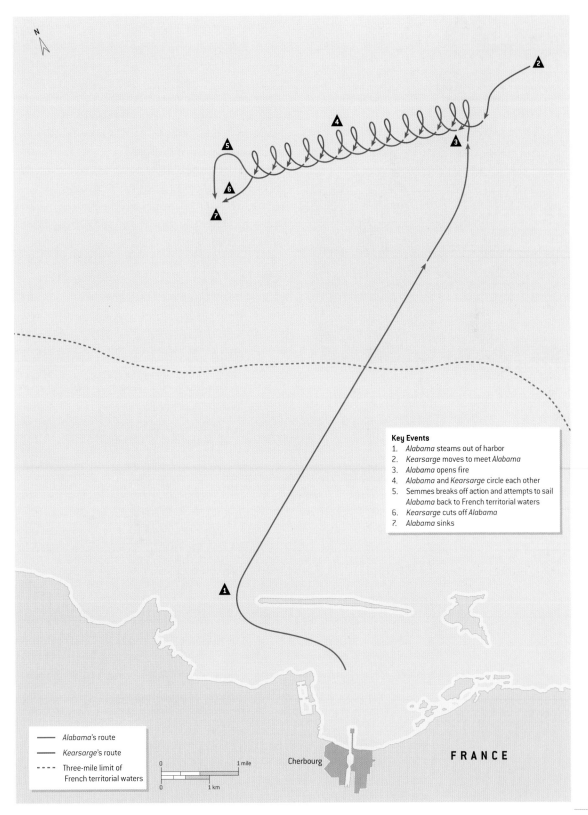

Key Events

1. *Alabama* steams out of harbor
2. *Kearsarge* moves to meet *Alabama*
3. *Alabama* opens fire
4. *Alabama* and *Kearsarge* circle each other
5. Semmes breaks off action and attempts to sail *Alabama* back to French territorial waters
6. *Kearsarge* cuts off *Alabama*
7. *Alabama* sinks

—— *Alabama*'s route

—— *Kearsarge*'s route

‐ ‐ ‐ Three-mile limit of French territorial waters

0   1 mile

0   1 km

Cherbourg

FRANCE

John McIntosh Kell served as Semmes's first lieutenant on both *Sumter* and *Alabama*. Along with Semmes he was rescued by *Deerhound* and taken to Britain after the battle with *Kearsarge*. (AC)

For the next four days the two ships prepared for combat. Both ships struck unnecessary masts and yards, reducing their rigs to topmasts and yards. Unnecessary material was sent below or ashore. Semmes left the contents of *Alabama*'s strongbox (including all of the cash aboard and bonds accumulated from unburned prizes) ashore, and transferred his collection of captured chronometers to a friendly British yacht.

The French – adhering to the letter of neutrality law – blocked all attempts by both sides to augment crew from French ports. *Kearsarge* sought American sailors released by *Alabama* when it arrived, but the French prohibited them from boarding. *Rappahannock*, another Confederate raider, was in Cherbourg, and the French forbade even visits to *Alabama* from that ship. However, two of *Alabama*'s master's mates, Prussians who had joined *Alabama* in Capetown, had departed for home leave after *Alabama* docked at Cherbourg; as part of *Alabama*'s crew when it arrived in port, they were allowed to rejoin the ship.

Semmes filled his coal bunkers, more for the protection the coal would offer his engine during the fight than for the operational radius it would give him. Coaling took longer than expected, and *Alabama* was not ready to sail until the afternoon of Friday, June 17. Semmes decided to sail the following morning, but Saturday dawned with roiling seas and foul weather. He remained in port, awaiting calmer seas.

Sunday, June 19 dawned clear. *Alabama*'s crew was up by then, making preparations to sail. *Kearsarge*, waiting outside the breakwater, observed sparks rising from *Alabama*'s smokestack. At 7.30am *Alabama* raised steam, but it did not raise anchor until 9.00am. *Alabama* finally left Cherbourg at 9.45am, preceded by *Deerhound*, a British yacht whose owner wished to watch the fight, and *Couronne*, a French ironclad, sent to enforce French neutrality. Pilot boats trailed the raider, carrying additional spectators.

Winslow was holding church service when *Alabama* cleared the breakwater. He ended the service, calling the crew to quarters and clearing the ship for action. He then pointed *Kearsarge* north, sailing away from the French coast. Winslow wanted to draw *Alabama* far enough from the French shore that it could not easily reenter territorial waters if things went badly for the Confederates. Both ships sailed northeast until Alabama was 6 miles from the French coast – 3 miles past the limit of French authority.

At 10.50am, 7 miles from the French coast, Winslow ordered *Kearsarge* to port, back to *Alabama*, readying its starboard broadside. As *Kearsarge* finished its 180-degree turn, *Alabama* turned to port, presenting its starboard side to the oncoming Union cruiser. At 1,200 yards Semmes opened the action, firing the six guns on his starboard

battery at *Kearsarge*. All shots from this first broadside went high. It was 10.57am.

Winslow continued towards *Alabama* receiving two more broadsides. These also missed. At 11.00am Winslow finally turned his starboard broadside towards *Alabama*, and opened fire at 900 yards. Both captains now attempted to cross the bow of their opponent. The result was that the two ships began circling each other, like two prizefighters stalking their opponents in a boxing ring. The ships began this circling at a range of 800 yards, but slowly closed as the battle continued.

A general action now commenced with *Alabama* firing as rapidly as its guns could be loaded. *Kearsarge's* crew fired more deliberately, taking time before firing their guns. Both sides concentrated fire on their opponent's quarterdeck. *Kearsarge* found the range early and began landing hits almost immediately. Ten to 15 minutes after *Kearsarge* opened fire, it shot away *Alabama's* mizzen gaff, carrying away the Confederate ensign. Semmes had a fresh one raised on the mizzen top.

Alabama's fire was less accurate than *Kearsarge's* throughout the action. It took 18 minutes before it landed a shot. A shell from *Alabama's* after pivot exploded over *Kearsarge's* quarterdeck, injuring three sailors operating the Union cruiser's after pivot. It was the first of only a dozen hits on *Kearsarge's* hull, and one of the few shells fired that actually exploded. This included a shell fired from *Alabama's* forward Blakely rifle that struck *Kearsarge* under its counter, failed to explode, and then lodged in the *Kearsarge's* sternpost. By then it was clear that half of *Alabama's* shells were duds. Halfway through the battle, Semmes switched to solid shot, abandoning use of shell.

By this time, *Alabama* had taken serious damage from *Kearsarge's* fire, especially its 11in Dahlgrens. While *Alabama's* shot flew over *Kearsarge*, *Kearsarge's* Dahlgren crews aimed at the waterline of *Alabama*, landing hits amidships. One shell struck home

An early phase of the battle between *Alabama* and *Kearsarge* is shown in this Currier & Ives print. It inaccurately depicts the combatants under sail. (LOC)

COMMANDER'S VIEW – *ALABAMA*'S QUARTERDECK

Raphael Semmes hoped to board and capture *Kearsarge* intact when he offered to fight the cruiser. That proved impossible while *Kearsarge* was able to maneuver. Semmes now plans to sink *Kearsarge*. The two ships are now trading broadsides at a range of 600 yards. Semmes tries to cross *Kearsarge*'s bow or stern, while Winslow, aboard *Kearsarge*, attempts to do the same to *Alabama*. Instead the two ships are circling each other. At the point shown in this plate, the two ships are completing their third revolution.

Alabama's crew are handling their guns rapidly, yet to no apparent effect. Semmes can see the quarterdeck 32-pounder's crew working their weapon, firing yet again. Few shells seem to be exploding. Kell and Semmes worried about the quality of the shells before the battle as the magazine was located between the engine room and the water distiller – a protected, but high-humidity location. Kell and Semmes have been discussing the issue, and Semmes has just ordered the guns to switch to solid shot. Suddenly, *Alabama* shudders under the impact of a fresh hit amidships. Semmes and his staff look forward where they see a pillar of coal-dust erupting from the starboard bunker. The hit, not instantly fatal, causes leaks that will eventually flood *Alabama*.

COMMANDER'S VIEW – *KEARSARGE*'S QUARTERDECK

John Winslow vainly chased Confederate raiders for eighteen months. When he steamed to Cherbourg, he expected another long, weary wait outside a neutral port for a Confederate cruiser that would escape him during a dark night. Instead, *Alabama*, the most notorious raider of all, came out to challenge him. Now *Kearsarge* is locked in a battle with its foe. The two ships are circling each other, vainly attempting to cross the other's bow or stern.

Yet Winslow now has few complaints. *Alabama*'s fire is going high. By this point only a few hits have landed on *Kearsarge*, and done little damage. While some of *Alabama*'s shells have exploded – including one that injured several members of the aft Dahlgren's crew – others have not, serving merely as lighter hollow shot.

His crew is firing deliberately, taking time to aim each shot carefully. As *Kearsarge* completes its third revolution of the deadly merry-go-round track the ships are following, Winslow notices something. He points it out to his first lieutenant, James Thornton. A black cloud is rising amidships on *Alabama*. One of *Kearsarge*'s Dahlgrens has landed a serious hit.

The final stage of the battle – *Kearsarge* crossing the sinking *Alabama*'s bow to prevent the Confederate ship from reaching neutral waters. (USN)

below the waterline, exploding against *Alabama*'s coal bunker. The coal did its job of protecting the engine room, but a massive cloud of coal-dust erupted, marking the hit, which started seams in *Alabama*'s hull.

More hits followed. The crew of the after Blakely took so many casualties that Semmes used the crew from the quarterdeck 32-pounder to replace the losses. By this stage, the after pivot – the 8in smoothbore – seemed the only effective gun; the 32-pounders seemed to be doing little damage, and the Blakely rifle forward was overheating, reducing its rate of fire. Late in the battle Semmes switched back to shell.

At 45 minutes into the battle *Alabama* took another 11in hit below the waterline. *Alabama* was now taking in water at an alarming rate, threatening the engine room. Word was passed from the engine room that it was in danger of flooding. As *Alabama* was about to begin its seventh circle, Semmes ordered the ship to starboard, breaking away from the fight, and attempting to turn *Alabama* toward the French coast and safety. In response, Winslow straightened his path, and steered to cut *Alabama* off from the coast.

By then, *Alabama*'s engine room was flooding. Kell, the executive officer, reported that the ship would sink within 15 minutes. Semmes began setting his fore-and-aft sails in an attempt to run for the coast, but saw that *Kearsarge* was between France and the now-sinking *Alabama*. Just 400 yards away, *Kearsarge* raked *Alabama* with its large Dahlgrens. Realizing that escape was impossible, Semmes ordered *Alabama*'s colors struck. It was noon.

Kearsarge continued firing after Semmes struck his colors, and Semmes afterward claimed this was a deliberate violation of the customs of war. In fact, it is more likely that it was due to the fog of war. *Alabama* had been without a flag early in the battle, after *Kearsarge* shot away *Alabama*'s gaff. Just after Semmes ordered the flag lowered, *Alabama*'s forward guns fired. Rather than recognizing the act of surrender, Winslow assumed that he had shot away *Alabama*'s ensign once again, and therefore continued firing. *Kearsarge* fired five more shots before two sailors aboard *Alabama* raised a white flag, and Winslow ordered fire to cease.

By then, Semmes was getting his crew off the sinking *Alabama*. Two of *Alabama*'s boats, both on the sheltered port side, survived the battle and were already in the water. Semmes ordered one boat to go to *Kearsarge* with *Alabama*'s wounded and request assistance. *Kearsarge* lowered boats to rescue *Alabama*'s crew, but it too had only two undamaged boats. *Alabama* sank a few minutes later, 70 minutes after the battle started, leaving the surviving crew struggling in the water.

Deerhound, which had been watching the battle, steamed up and offered to help. Winslow asked the yacht to pick up *Alabama*'s survivors. The yacht steamed into the group of survivors, pulled 41 men aboard and then sailed to Southampton, England, without waiting to rescue the rest. *Deerhound*'s haul included 14 officers (including Semmes and Kell) and eight petty officers. Winslow's officers, seeing the ship leaving the scene, urged Winslow to fire a shot across its bow, to force it to stay. Winslow refused, claiming that no English gentleman would take legitimate prisoners from the scene of a battle.

The remaining survivors were pulled aboard *Kearsarge* and several French pilot boats that were on the scene. Of *Alabama*'s crew, 16 men were drowned; nine had been killed during the battle and 22 were wounded. A total of 68 crew members ended up as prisoners aboard *Kearsarge*; they were later landed in France, and paroled.

OVERLEAF: *WACHUSETT* **CAPTURES** *FLORIDA*

Commander Napoleon Collins, commanding *Wachusett*, did not plan to battle in a neutral harbor. He intended to sink *Florida* by ramming it. As with other Confederate raiders built on plans for civilian ships, *Florida* had lighter scantlings than a warship. Collins hoped one good hit with *Wachusett*'s prow would settle the issue decisively. It could then be explained away as an "accident." However, the hit was only a glancing blow, which failed to open *Florida*'s hull. Then *Wachusett*'s second-in-command ordered cannons fired. An exchange of fire resulted, as shown in this plate. Collins knows he will get the blame for violating neutrality – he now thinks he might as well take *Florida* while he can, and have something positive to show for his actions.

IMPOSED COMBAT: *FLORIDA* vs *WACHUSETT*

With the loss of *Alabama*, the sale of *Georgia*, and *Rappahannock* trapped at Cherbourg with useless engines, *Florida* was the sole remaining Confederate commerce raider at large in the fall of 1864. *Florida* had sailed from Brest, France, in February 1864, after receiving the type of refit Semmes had sought for *Alabama*. Union Navy officials were eager to run *Florida* to ground and end the cruiser menace. Initially *Wachusett*, a sister of *Kearsarge*, received instructions in July to search for *Florida*. *Kearsarge* joined the chase that fall, diverted while returning to the United States after three years overseas.

Wachusett found *Florida* first – or, rather, *Florida* found *Wachusett*. *Wachusett*'s captain, Napoleon Collins, had taken his ship to Brazilian waters, seeking the raider off the bulge of Brazil. Collins stopped at Bahia, Brazil, for supplies and coal. At 9.00pm on October 4, 1864, while *Wachusett* rode at anchor in Bahia, an unknown steamer cruised into port. Collins sent a boat to discover the stranger's identity. It was *Florida*.

Her captain, Lieutenant Commander C. Manigault Morris, had put in to take on stores and replace a leaking condenser tube in *Florida*'s steam engine. Morris was unaware of the Union warship's presence when he entered Bahia. It was only on the following day that morning light revealed that *Florida*'s neighbor, moored only a quarter-mile away, was a Union warship – though the crew of the boat *Wachusett* sent over to *Florida* identified the warship already anchored at Bahia as the British warship HMS *Curlew*.

Florida sailing in company with *Wachusett*, following the capture of *Florida* in Bahia, Brazil. (LOC)

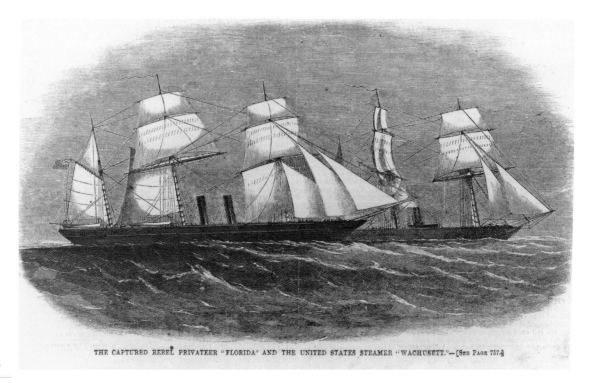

THE CAPTURED REBEL PRIVATEER "FLORIDA" AND THE UNITED STATES STEAMER "WACHUSETT."—[See Page 757.]

Brazil was neutral in the conflict between the Confederacy and the United States, and the Brazilian authorities immediately sought assurances from both parties that neither would initiate hostilities. Morris was also invited to move *Florida* deeper in the harbor, with a Brazilian warship between the two combatants. Morris declined this offer, preferring to remain where he was rather than delay repairs by moving his ship.

Collins was in a situation previously experienced by other Union captains. There were numerous instances where Union cruisers had trapped Confederate raiders in neutral ports. Each time the raider had evaded the blockader and continued its cruise. Collins was determined that this would not happen again. He sent a written challenge to Morris, inviting the ship to fight a duel outside Brazilian waters similar to that between *Alabama* and *Kearsarge*.

Morris refused to accept the challenge, returning letters sent unopened. Morris claimed they were improperly addressed to the "sloop *Florida*" rather than "CSS *Florida*" – the latter term implicitly recognized Confederate sovereignty, unacceptable to a United States Navy officer. Even had Morris read the letter – he was soon aware of its contents, regardless of whether he had read it – he would have been ill-advised to accept the challenge. Defeating *Wachusett* might have gained transitory glory, but any damage sustained would have made continuing *Florida*'s cruise impossible.

By sunset on October 6, it was apparent that Collins would receive no reply to his challenge. He decided to take matters into his own hands, developing a plan that offered sufficient plausible deniability to deflect neutral anger. Collins would shift anchor – during the middle of the night – "accidentally" ramming and sinking *Florida* during this evolution. He began making preparations, reducing the ship's rig to its absolute minimum, striking the upper masts, and pulling in the jib boom.

Morris may have viewed these preparations as an indication that Collins planned a long harbor stay, as *Wachusett*'s rig made cruising under sail impossible. He may also have been convinced that the port's neutrality was sufficient protection against attack. On October 6 Morris gave half his crew leave, allowing them to remain ashore that night. Only 83 members of *Florida*'s crew were aboard as dusk fell. A total of 75 others, including Morris, were ashore.

At 3.00am on October 7, *Wachusett* raised steam and slipped its anchor. At this point, however, Collins's plan began unraveling. Inadequate preparation by *Wachusett*'s first officer, Lieutenant Commander L. A. Beardslee, prevented *Wachusett*'s anchor chain from being released silently. The noise alerted those remaining aboard *Florida* to the fact that something was up, and the senior officer aboard ordered the hands to station. A few minutes later, *Wachusett* loomed out of the dark, and struck the anchored *Florida* just aft of the mizzenmast.

The ramming was mishandled. *Wachusett* struck only a glancing blow, failing to stave in *Florida*'s hull. The blow was sufficient to knock down *Florida*'s mizzenmast and flatten the bulwarks where the ship was struck. In turn, the falling mizzenmast pulled down the main topmast, the main yard, and the awnings spread over the quarterdeck and between the main and mizzenmasts. The canvas collapsed, covering the crew on the after half of the ship.

As Collins backed *Wachusett* away for another ramming attempt, the fig leaf of plausible deniability abruptly vanished. Beardslee thought he heard pistol shots from *Florida*. Against orders, he ordered *Wachusett*'s bow guns to fire. They blazed out, firing two shots at nothing in particular. Then the two ships began exchanging small-arms fire. Believing that having openly violated Brazilian neutrality there was nothing more to lose, Collins decided that he might as well have a prize to show for it. He called upon *Florida* to surrender. When Lieutenant Thomas Porter, then commanding aboard *Florida*, refused, Collins threatened to resume fire.

Florida, with half its crew ashore, and the deck in disorder, was unable to fight. After consulting with the remaining officers aboard, Porter surrendered *Florida*, conditionally and under protest. Moreover, 15 crewmen aboard *Florida* decided they would rather take their chances with the sea than as Yankee prisoners. Jumping overboard, they swam for shore. Six made it; nine drowned.

Collins boarded *Florida*, took the remaining crew prisoner, tied a hawser to his prize, and towed *Florida* out to sea. By now, Brazilian authorities were aware of the battle. They fired three shots at the ships before they sailed out of range of shore batteries, but none hit. In the morning Brazil sent two warships – a paddle steamer and a sailing sloop of war – in pursuit, but Collins outran them.

STATISTICS AND ANALYSIS

While victory did not necessarily go to the larger broadside in these Civil War single-ship actions, it always favored the side with the heaviest guns. Furthermore, it did not go to the side with the highest rate of fire, but rather to the side that landed the most hits and hit hardest. Accuracy required aiming.

Table 1 (overleaf) shows the guns mounted and broadsides carried by the ships in each battle. The victorious ship in each battle is highlighted. As can be seen there was little variation in the total number of guns carried by each ship, and little variation between the numbers of guns each ship was capable of firing in one broadside. The biggest discrepancy in gun count was in the battle between *Alabama* and *Hatteras*. *Alabama* carried 33 percent more guns than *Hatteras* – eight guns to six. Even there, the broadside count was not that great – five guns to four. Similarly close ratios can be seen in the other two examples – eight guns to seven for *Alabama* vs *Kearsarge*, and eight guns to nine for *Florida* and *Wachusett*.

The real difference lay in the size of the guns carried, and the subsequent effect on broadside, particularly in the two battles settled by gunfire. Its two large pivots allowed *Alabama* to throw a broadside weight twice that of *Hatteras*, while *Kearsarge*'s 11in Dahlgren pivots – each throwing a 133lb shell – gave *Kearsarge* a weight of broadside greater by one-third than *Alabama*, even though its total number of broadside guns was 20 percent smaller than that of *Alabama*.

Broadside weight does not tell the whole story. The size of the shots striking home also affected the damage. The guns that fired smaller projectiles – the traditional 32-pounder smoothbores carried by most ships as broadside guns, and the 30- and 20-pounder Parrotts used as chase guns – were satisfactory when used to stop unarmed

Table 1				
Battle	Ship	Guns aboard	Guns fired in a broadside	Total broadside weight (pounds)
Alabama vs Hatteras, January 11, 1863	Alabama	One 7in Blakely rifle, one 68-pounder Blakely smoothbore, six 32-pounder smoothbores	One 7in Blakely rifle, one 68-pounder Blakely smoothbore, three 32-pounder smoothbores	242
	Hatteras	One 30-pounder Parrott rifle, one 20-pounder Parrott rifle, four 32-pounder smoothbores	One 30-pounder Parrott rifle, one 20-pounder Parrott rifle, two 32-pounder smoothbores	114
Alabama vs Kearsarge, June 19, 1864	Alabama	One 7in Blakely rifle, one 68-pounder Blakely smoothbore, six 32-pounder smoothbores	One 7in Blakely rifle, one 68-pounder Blakely smoothbore, four 32-pounder smoothbores*	274
	Kearsarge	Two 11in Dahlgren smoothbores, one 30-pounder Parrott rifle, four 32-pounder smoothbores	Two 11in Dahlgren smoothbores, one 30-pounder Parrott rifle, two 32-pounder smoothbores	360
Florida vs Wachusett, October 7, 1864	Florida	Two 7in Blakely rifles, six 6in Blakely rifles	Two 7in Blakely rifles, three 6in Blakely rifles	350
	Wachusett	Three 100-pounder Parrott rifles, two 30-pounder Parrott rifles, four 32-pounder smoothbores	Two 100-pounder Parrott rifles, two 30-pounder Parrott rifles, two 32-pounder smoothbores	324

* *Alabama* remounted its 32-pounders so that two could fire on both sides

merchant vessels, whether oceangoing Yankee clippers or Rebel blockade runners. They apparently did little damage to warships in combat, even when firing explosive shell rather than solid shot.

When they hit home these projectiles had difficulty penetrating an intact wooden hull on the first strike. Penetration with those guns depended upon hitting the same spot more than once. The first shot would weaken the timbers, while subsequent hits could shatter the weakened wood. In the Napoleonic era a ship fired solid shot from dozens of 32-pounder guns against the sides of an opponent for hours at ranges that were too close for a shot to miss, yet would fail to reduce a ship to a sinking condition.

Explosive shells accelerated the process, but the charge carried by shells fired from 32-pounders or smaller guns carried too little explosive to cause truly decisive damage against a sturdy ship with one shot, unless it hit at a critical location, such as the rudder. An empirical demonstration of this comes from *Alabama*'s fight with *Hatteras*. *Hatteras* struck *Alabama*'s sides several times during the battle, but none of the hits caused serious damage. Some of the hits went unrepaired, the scars a source of pride to *Alabama*'s crew, who pointed them out to visitors.

Larger shells did considerable damage, however. *Hatteras* was torn apart by *Alabama*'s guns. Three hits were sufficient to reduce the paddle-wheeler to a sinking condition. One shell penetrated into the hold, exploded, and started a fire. A second went through the side of the ship and punctured the cylinder of the steam engine. A third drove through the side of the ship, penetrating through two bulkheads and passing through the sick bay before exploding. Those shells were almost certainly fired by *Alabama*'s large pivot guns.

Similarly, most of the damage to *Alabama* during its battle with *Kearsarge* appears to have been done by the 11in Dahlgrens. Each hit by an 11in shell exploded with enough force to tear a 2ft to 3ft hole in *Alabama*'s side. The fatal damage appears to have been done by either two or three shells that struck near the waterline. The most immediately fatal of them seems to have been a hit late in the battle – perhaps during the fifth or sixth circle performed by the two ships – which admitted enough water to sink *Alabama* within 20 minutes. It is hard to determine whether earlier hits would also have eventually sunk the ship, as damage was cumulative.

Sinking a ship required hitting it. That increased the importance of accurate gunnery, especially since a single shot now had the potential to sink a ship. Rate of fire took a back seat to marksmanship. Table 2 shows the accuracy of each ship's fire during battle. In the two battles decided by gunnery, the victor had a greater accuracy of fire.

Commander James Thornton was *Kearsarge*'s executive officer during its battle with *Alabama*. (AC)

Table 2				
Battle	**Ship**	**Shots fired**	**Total hits**	**Hit percentage**
Alabama vs *Hatteras*, January 11, 1863	*Alabama*	32–36	10–15	28–47%
	Hatteras	50	4–6	8–12%
Alabama vs *Kearsarge*, June 19, 1864	*Alabama*	Approx. 300	28	8–10%
	Kearsarge	173	Unknown, at least 30	15–25%
Florida vs *Wachusett*, October 7, 1864	*Florida*	0	0	n/a
	Wachusett	2	0	0%

THE ROLE OF THE *DEERHOUND*

One enduring controversy about the battle of Cherbourg was whether *Deerhound*'s rescue of Semmes and his officers had been arranged before the battle. Semmes, his officers, and the captain and owner of *Deerhound* all said not — immediately after the battle and long afterwards. Yet the composition of those rescued by *Deerhound* and spirited to Britain, out of reach of the Union Navy, seems too convenient without prearrangement: 14 officers (including the captain and first lieutenant), eight petty officers, and only 19 sailors or firemen. *Alabama* had 146 men aboard at the battle, including 20 officers and 24 petty officers.

Equally curious was Winslow's reaction. Despite pleas, he refused to force *Deerhound* to stop by firing on it. Afterward he claimed he did not believe an English gentleman would be mean enough to run. But *Deerhound* relieved Winslow of inconvenient guests, especially Semmes and Kell. Had they been taken and sent to the United States it is possible that both could have been hanged as pirates — an outcome Winslow was unlikely to wish on an old shipmate. He might have welcomed what happened, despite later denials. As it was, Winslow incurred the ire of the Navy by releasing most of his prisoners on parole.

Commander Napoleon Collins violated international law when he fired on *Florida* in a neutral harbor. (NHHC)

Many numbers in this table are approximations. Semmes did not report ammunition usage in either of his battles. The estimate for the shots fired in the battle between *Alabama* and *Hatteras* was derived from my estimate of the time it takes to reload, run-out, and fire the cannon used on *Alabama* over the reported time of the battle. The estimate for his second battle is based on the Union estimate that *Alabama* was firing twice as fast as *Kearsarge* (the higher rate of fire was confirmed by Confederate and neutral accounts of the battle). Rounds fired by *Hatteras* were taken from Blake's report. Hits landed by *Alabama* on *Hatteras* are an estimate by me, based on the damage reported by Blake.

Hits by *Alabama* on *Kearsarge* were enumerated in various *Kearsarge* after-action reports. Only half of these hits struck the hull. *Hatteras*'s hits on *Alabama* come from Semmes's report ("We received a few shot holes from the enemy, doing no damage"). The number of hits landed on *Alabama* by *Kearsarge* is my guess based on damage reported and the casualties taken by *Alabama*'s crew. It is probably too low. *Alabama*'s 14 hits on *Kearsarge*'s hull inflicted three casualties; 30 of *Alabama*'s crew were killed during the battle. Even within these limitations, the available data shows a general trend. The victorious ship significantly fired fewer rounds, while scoring a greater number of hits.

Table 2 also suggests that *Alabama*'s gunnery deteriorated during its cruise. There was probably some drop-off in gunnery efficiency, but it is not necessarily as great as

While large shell-firing guns made boarding actions obsolete, sailors still trained for them. This drawing shows cutlass drill aboard *Alabama*. (AC)

THE STERNPOST HIT

During the battle, a shell from *Alabama*'s Blakely rifle struck *Kearsarge* under its counter and lodged in its sternpost. It failed to explode. One of the biggest "what-ifs" of the battle is what would have happened had it exploded.

Semmes claims that it would have given *Alabama* the victory. This is possibly, but not necessarily, the case. Semmes states that it had a percussion fuse; so if the shell had exploded on contact it might never have reached the sternpost, instead exploding where it hit the counter. The hole would have been well above the waterline. This would have caused serious, but not necessarily fatal damage.

Had it exploded after lodging in the sternpost, the hole created would probably have been above the waterline. It would have destroyed the rudder, affecting steering. Yet even this would not necessarily have been fatal. *Kearsarge* could have steered using sails, although it would have been less maneuverable than *Alabama*.

Even if the hit had proved fatal, it might not have altered *Alabama*'s ultimate fate. *Alabama* had already taken serious damage by the time it fired that shot. At least one 11in shell had already exploded below the waterline. The battle might have ended with both ships sunk. Even with *Kearsarge* sunk, *Alabama* would have been too badly damaged to resume its cruise. With France unwilling to anger the United States, *Alabama* would probably have ended the war moored at Cherbourg, unable to sail without repairs and unable to get those repairs.

The sternpost of *Kearsarge* with its unexploded shell from *Alabama* was preserved and is on display at the Navy Museum in Washington, DC. (NHHC)

these numbers indicate. *Alabama*'s first duel was fought at much closer ranges than its second duel. Alabama was firing at *Hatteras* at distances no greater than 400 yards. Sometimes it was only 50 yards from its target. *Alabama* was no closer than 400 yards from *Kearsarge* throughout that battle, and was only that close at the end, when *Alabama*'s engines were gone. Most of the battle was fought at ranges between 500 and 800 yards.

There was another reason for *Alabama*'s relatively poor accuracy during its second battle. In the last half of the cruise, to preserve shot and shell, Semmes conducted significantly less live-fire practice or aiming at marks than he had done in the initial months of the ship's voyage. Additionally, during the last leg of the cruise, from Capetown to Cherbourg, there were fewer opportunities to exercise his guns. There were almost no prizes. Nor did *Alabama*'s crew consist of picked man-of-war men. They were a typical collection of British merchant seamen in the right place to have been recruited for *Alabama*. Some had served aboard Royal Navy warships, but without incessant drill – drill that Winslow of *Kearsarge* could conduct, because he had a supply of replacement ammunition – accuracy would suffer. This difference gave *Kearsarge* an important advantage in the battle.

Another issue with *Alabama*'s fighting ability was the quality of *Alabama*'s shells. When Semmes took *Rockingham* as a prize, on April 22, 1864, he used it for gunnery practice. Five shells were fired at *Rockingham*. None exploded. Either the fuses that detonated the shells or the powder within the shells had deteriorated. Semmes ordered his gunner to replace all fuses in his arsenal, but that only partially fixed the problem. Fewer than half the shells that struck *Kearsarge* exploded, including the dud that lodged in the sternpost.

Semmes later claimed that *Kearsarge*'s improvised chain armor also contributed to *Alabama*'s defeat, in that *Alabama*'s guns could not penetrate this armored belt. *Alabama* scored only three hits on this part of the ship – one solid shot and two shells. None of these shots, even had they penetrated, would have damaged the engines. All hit at or near the deck level. This armor might have made a difference had *Alabama* landed hits over the machinery area, low in the hull. Since this portion of *Kearsarge* went untouched, it is hard to see how the armor's presence altered the battle. Bad gunnery to a greater extent than bad ammunition or Yankee armor doomed *Alabama* in its last fight. *Alabama*'s fire went high, most shots flying harmlessly over *Kearsarge*. Of the shots that landed, half hit the rigging. The remainder hit high on the hull.

The destructive power of shells and steam propulsion created another major change from earlier wars. Boarding actions – against warships, especially – were obsolete. A ship that could maneuver could not be boarded unless surprised. Even when a ship could be boarded – because it had been battered to a standstill, or like *Florida* surprised at anchor – there was no reason to board. *Florida* surrendered to *Wachusett* not because its acting commander feared being boarded, or because Collins intended to board *Florida*. Rather, it was *Wachusett*'s battery trained upon *Florida* ready to fire, with *Florida* unable to reply, that necessitated surrender.

The officers of *Kearsarge*, shown here posing as a group after the battle with *Alabama*, were a cross-section of the United States Navy's Civil War officer corps – long-service regulars augmented by volunteers from merchant service. (NHHC)

AFTERMATH

The three duels fought between Confederate raiders and Union cruisers continued to have repercussions even after the gunfire ceased. They would be repeatedly re-fought in the memoirs of the participants and their partisans.

Wachusett's capture of *Florida* had the most immediate repercussions. The incident caused a diplomatic uproar. Brazil sent a warship to the United States with a formal protest and a demand for *Florida*'s restoration. Collins was court-martialed for violating Brazilian neutrality, convicted, and dismissed from the Navy. The Navy agreed to return *Florida* to Brazil. However, before the transfer could occur, *Florida* was again "accidentally" rammed – this time by an Army transport – in Chesapeake Bay and allowed to sink. Brazil settled for reparations and a sincere apology. Collins was eventually restored to duty and seniority after the war's end, once tempers cooled.

Both Winslow and Semmes were fêted as heroes after their battle, the loser perhaps more than the victor. Winslow – whose career had stalled prior to assuming command of *Kearsarge* – now found its progression restored. It was perhaps too late for him to appreciate the honors given him. His cruise as *Kearsarge*'s captain ruined his always-fragile health. Instead of passing to obscure retirement, where he could have enjoyed time with his family and recuperated, he was pushed into continued active duty, which further degraded his health.

Semmes had a rockier postwar career. Hostility to him in the Reconstruction South

Found by French divers in 1984, *Alabama*'s wreck has been of great interest to marine archaeologists. A United States Navy researcher is shown here with artifacts recovered from the wreck, including a brass hose nozzle. (USN)

made it impossible for him to hold a job. He also endured a brief imprisonment, and the dissipation of his prewar savings. Eventually he recovered a measure of financial security as a lecturer and author.

Controversy dogged the battle of Cherbourg. Winslow accused the Confederates rescued by *Deerhound* and *Deerhound*'s crew of bad faith for fleeing the scene after surrender. The act was contrary to customs of war. Semmes was even more pugnacious, claiming that he had been defeated because he had been fighting an "armored" ship. In a way, Semmes's memoirs were a masterpiece – describing the various ruses, precautions, and deceptions that he himself practiced as examples of shrewd judgment and manly boldness, while depicting all similar ruses, precautions, and deceptions exercised by the Yankees as examples of mean cowardice and calculating scheming.

Confederate commerce raiding proved strategically barren. While costly to the North during the war, the cost fell mainly on the civilian owners of the cargos captured and ships burned. Since the United States during the Civil War – unlike Great Britain during two World Wars – did not depend upon foreign trade for survival, no number of Yankee ships captured could have forced the North to quit. Ultimately the cost fell on Britain as much as the United States. Construction of Confederate ships in Britain led to charges that Great Britain had violated neutrality laws. Britain agreed to third-party arbitration of American claims for damages following the war; an international tribunal found in favor of the United States in 1872, and Britain paid a $15.5 million settlement, called the *Alabama* Claims, to the United States.

While prized by the United States and the Navy as a symbol of victory over the Confederacy, *Kearsarge* ran aground on Roncador Reef, and could not be salvaged. (LOC)

FURTHER READING

Few Civil War maritime subjects have been as enthusiastically written about as the operations of the Confederate and Union cruisers. A romance is attached to the actions of captains operating independently of outside authority over long periods, one that attaches to captains of both sides. Popular accounts are not always reliable – even those written by participants, who often put a gloss on their activities. That said, the starting point for any examination of these actions is the first-person accounts.

Raphael Semmes wrote two memoirs – *The Cruise of the Alabama and the Sumter*, originally published in 1864 in Britain from Semmes's logbooks, and the postwar *Memoirs of Service Afloat During the War Between the States*, which first appeared in 1869. Both are available online, the former at Project Gutenberg (<http://www.gutenberg.org/>), and the latter at the University of Michigan's Making of America archives (<http://quod.lib.umich.edu/m/moagrp/>). Other Confederate participants, including James Bulloch, Arthur Sinclair, and John McIntosh Kell, also wrote memoirs.

On the Union side, first-person accounts are sparser. However, one Marine aboard *Kearsarge* wrote an account of its cruise (in a long epic poem), as did William Badlam, one of *Kearsarge*'s engineers. His prose account is available online (at <http://suvcw.org/mollus/warpapers/MAv1a2p11.htm>).

The most comprehensive recent account of both ships' activities remains William Marvel's well-researched *The Alabama and Kearsarge: The Sailor's Civil War* (University of North Carolina Press, Chapel Hill, NC, 1996). Also worth reading is Stephen Fox's *Wolf of the Deep: Raphael Semmes and the Notorious Confederate Raider CSS Alabama* (Alfred A. Knopf, New York, NY, 2007).

There are many outstanding books about the Confederate raiders, but I would like to mention Stephen Chapin Kinnaman's *The Most Perfect Cruiser* (Dog Ear Publishing, Indianapolis, IN, 2009), an excellent account of the building of *Alabama*. Others are listed below.

Accounts of the warships of the Union Navy are harder to find, but two of Donald Canney's are worth reading: *The Old Steam Navy: Volume I. Frigates, Sloops, and Gunboats, 1815–1885* (Naval Institute Press, Annapolis, MD, 1992), and *Mr. Lincoln's Navy* (Naval Institute Press, Annapolis, MD, 1998).

Although the battles are done their memory lives on. Mobile, Alabama, erected this monument to Raphael Semmes shortly after his death. [LOC]

A partial list of works I used also includes:

Bowcock, Andrew, *CSS Alabama: Anatomy of a Confederate Raider*, Chatham Publishing, London, 2003

Hill, Jim Dan, *Sea Dogs of the Sixties: Farragut and Seven Contemporaries*, A. S. Barnes & Co., New York, NY, 1961

Johnson, Robert U., and Buel, Clarence C., *Battles and Leaders of the Civil War, Vol. 4*, The Century Co., New York, NY, 1888

Owsely, Frank L. Jr., *The C.S.S. Florida, Her Building and Operations,* University of Alabama Press, Tuscaloosa, AL, 2002

Ringle, Dennis J., *Life in Mr. Lincoln's Navy*, Naval Institute Press, Annapolis, MD, 1998

Rush, Richard, and Woods, Robert, *Official Records of the Union and Confederate Navies in the War of the Rebellion, Series I: Vols 1–3*, United States Government Printing Office, Washington, DC, 1894–96

Tucker, Spencer, *Arming the Fleet, U.S. Navy Ordnance in the Muzzle-Loading Era*, United States Naval Institute Press, Annapolis, MD, 1989

INDEX